# Mindfulness

## in Plain English

# Mindfulness
## in Plain English

VENERABLE HENEPOLA GUNARATANA

Wisdom Publications
Boston

First published in Taiwan, 1991
This edition published in 1994

WISDOM PUBLICATIONS
361 Newbury Street
Boston, Massachusetts 02115

© Henepola Gunaratana 1991
All rights reserved.

*Library of Congress Cataloging-in-Publication Data*
Gunaratana, Henepola.
    Mindfulness in Plain English / Henepola Gunaratana.
        p. cm.
    ISBN 0–86171–064–9 (pbk.) :
    1. Vipasyana (Buddhism) 2. Meditation — Buddhism. I. Title
BQ5630.V5G86   1992
294.3' 443—dc20                                              92–33407

99  98  97  96  95

8   7   6   5   4

Set in Adobe Garamond by Wisdom Publications.

Designed and Illustrated by: L·J·SAWLiT

Wisdom Publications' books are printed on acid-free paper and meet the guidelines for permanence
and durability of the Committee on Production Guidelines for Book Longevity of the Council on
Library Resources.

Printed in the USA.

# TABLE OF CONTENTS

*The Publisher gratefully acknowledges the kind help of Jacalyn Bennett in sponsoring the publication of this book.*

# PREFACE

In my experience I have found that the most effective way to express something in order to make others understand is to use the simplest language. I have also learned from teaching that the more rigid the language the less effective it is. People do not respond to very stern and rigid language especially when we try to teach something which normally people don't engage in during daily life. Meditation appears to them as something that they cannot always do. As more people turn to meditation, they need more simplified instructions so they can practice by themselves without a teacher around. This book is the result of requests made by many meditators who need a very simple book written in ordinary colloquial language.

In preparing this book I have been helped by many of my friends. I am deeply grateful to all of them. Especially I would like to express my deepest appreciation and sincere gratitude to John M. Peddicord, Daniel J. Olmsted, Matthew Flickstein, Carol Flickstein, Patrick Hamilton, Genny Hamilton, Bill Mayne, Bhikkhu Dang Pham Jotika, and Bhikkhu Sona for their most valuable suggestions, comments, and criticisms of numerous points in preparing this book. Also thanks go to Reverend Sister Sama and Chris O'Keefe for their support in production efforts.

H. Gunaratana Mahathera

# INTRODUCTION

## AMERICAN BUDDHISM

The subject of this book is Vipassana meditation practice. Repeat, practice. This is a meditation manual, a nuts-and-bolts, step-by-step guide to Insight meditation. It is meant to be practical. It is meant for use.

There are already many comprehensive books on Buddhism as a philosophy, and on the theoretical aspects of Buddhist meditation. If you are interested in that material, we urge you to read those books. Many of them are excellent. This book is a "how to." It is written for those who actually want to meditate and especially for those who want to start now. There are very few qualified teachers of the Buddhist style of meditation in the United States of America. It is our intention to give you the basic data you need to get off to a flying start. Only those who follow the instructions given here can say whether we have succeeded or failed. Only those who actually meditate regularly and diligently can judge our effort. No book can possibly cover every problem that a meditator may run into. You will need to meet a qualified teacher eventually. In the meantime, however, these are the basic ground rules; a full understanding of these pages will take you a very long way.

There are many styles of meditation. Every major religious tradition has some sort of procedure which they call meditation, and the word is often very loosely used. Please understand that this volume deals exclusively with the Vipassana style of meditation as taught and practiced in South and

1

Southeast Asian Buddhism. It is often translated as Insight meditation, since the purpose of this system is to give the meditator insight into the nature of reality and accurate understanding of how everything works. Buddhism as a whole is quite different from the theological religions with which Westerners are most familiar. It is a direct entrance to a spiritual or divine realm without addressing deities or other "agents." Its flavor is intensely clinical, much more akin to what we would call psychology than to what we would usually call religion. It is an ever-ongoing investigation of reality, a microscopic examination of the very process of perception. Its intention is to pick apart the screen of lies and delusions through which we normally view the world, and thus to reveal the face of ultimate reality. Vipassana meditation is an ancient and elegant technique for doing just that.

Theravada Buddhism presents us with an effective system for exploring the deeper levels of the mind, down to the very root of consciousness itself. It also offers a considerable system of reverence and rituals in which those techniques are contained. This beautiful tradition is the natural result of its 2,500-year development within the highly traditional cultures of South and Southeast Asia.

In this volume, we will make every effort to separate the ornamental and the fundamental and to present only the naked plain truth itself. Those readers who are of a ritual bent may investigate the Theravada practice in other books, and will find there a vast wealth of customs and ceremony, a rich tradition full of beauty and significance. Those of a more clinical bent may use just the techniques themselves, applying them within whatever philosophical and emotional context they wish. The practice is the thing.

The distinction between Vipassana meditation and other styles of meditation is crucial and needs to be fully understood. Buddhism addresses two major types of meditation. They are different mental skills, modes of functioning or qualities of consciousness. In Pali, the original language of Theravada literature, they are called *Vipassana* and *Samatha*. *Vipassana* can be translated as "insight," a clear awareness of exactly what is happening as it happens. *Samatha* can be translated as "concentration" or "tranquility." It is a state in which the mind is brought to rest, focused only on one item and not allowed to wander. When this is done, a deep calm pervades body and mind, a state of tranquility which must be experienced to be understood. Most systems of meditation emphasize the *Samatha* component. The meditator focuses his mind upon some items, such as prayer, a certain type of box, a chant, a candle flame, a religious image or whatever, and excludes all other thoughts and perceptions from his consciousness. The result is a state of rapture which lasts until the meditator ends the session of sitting. It is beautiful, delightful, meaningful and alluring, but only temporary. *Vipassana* meditation addresses the other component, insight.

The Vipassana meditator uses his concentration as a tool by which his awareness can chip away at the wall of illusion which cuts him off from the living light of reality. It is a gradual process of ever-increasing awareness into the inner workings of reality itself. It takes years, but one day the meditator chisels through that wall and tumbles into the presence of light. The transformation is complete. It's called Liberation, and it's permanent. Liberation is the goal of all Buddhist systems of practice. But the routes to the attainment of that end are quite diverse.

There are an enormous number of distinct sects within Buddhism. But they divide into two broad streams of thought—Mahayana and Theravada. Mahayana Buddhism prevails throughout East Asia, shaping the cultures of China, Korea, Japan, Nepal, Tibet, and Vietnam. The most widely known of the Mahayana systems is Zen, practiced mainly in Japan, Korea, Vietnam, and the United States. The Theravada system of practice prevails in South and Southeast Asia in the countries of Sri Lanka, Thailand, Burma, Laos and Cambodia. This book deals with Theravada practice.

The traditional Theravada literature describes the techniques of both *Samatha* (concentration and tranquility of mind) and *Vipassana* (insight or clear awareness). There are forty different subjects of meditation described in the Pali literature. They are recommended as objects of concentration and as subjects of investigation leading to insight. But this is a basic manual, and we will limit our discussion to the most fundamental of those recommended objects—breathing. This book is an introduction to the attainment of mindfulness through bare attention to, and clear comprehension of, the whole process of breathing. Using the breath as his primary focus of attention, the meditator applies participatory observation to the entirety of his own perceptual universe. He learns to watch changes occurring in all physical experiences, in feelings and in perceptions. He learns to study his own mental activities and the fluctuations in the character of consciousness itself. All of these changes are occurring perpetually and are present in every moment of our experiences.

Meditation is a living activity, an inherently experiential activity. It cannot be taught as a purely scholastic subject.

The living heart of the process must come from the teacher's own personal experience. Nevertheless, there is a vast fund of codified material on the subject which is the product of some of the most intelligent and deeply illumined human beings ever to walk the earth. This literature is worthy of attention. Most of the points given in this book are drawn from the *Tipitaka*, which is the three-section collected work in which the Buddha's original teachings have been preserved. The *Tipitaka* is comprised of the Vinaya, the code of discipline for monks, nuns, and lay people; the Suttas, public discourses attributed to the Buddha; and the Abhidhamma, a set of deep psycho-philosophical teachings.

In the first century C.E., an eminent Buddhist scholar named Upatissa wrote the *Vimuttimagga (The Path of Freedom)*, in which he summarized the Buddha's teachings on meditation. In the fifth century C.E., another great Buddhist scholar named Buddhaghosa covered the same ground in a second scholastic thesis, the *Visuddhimagga (The Path of Purification)*, which is the standard text on meditation even today. Modern meditation teachers rely on the *Tipitaka* and upon their own personal experiences. It is our intention to present you with the clearest and most concise directions for Vipassana meditation available in the English language. This book offers you a foot in the door. It's up to you to take the first few steps on the road to the discovery of who you are and what it all means. It is a journey worth taking. We wish you success.

# CHAPTER 1

# MEDITATION: WHY BOTHER?

Meditation is not easy. It takes time and it takes energy. It also takes grit, determination, and discipline. It requires a host of personal qualities which we normally regard as unpleasant and which we like to avoid whenever possible. We can sum it all up in the American word *gumption*. Meditation takes gumption. It is certainly a great deal easier just to sit back and watch television. So why bother? Why waste all that time and energy when you could be out enjoying yourself? Why? Simple. Because you are human. And just because of the simple fact that you are human, you find yourself heir to an inherent unsatisfactoriness in life which simply will not go away. You can suppress it from your awareness for a time. You can distract yourself for hours on end, but it always comes back—usually when you least expect it. All of a sudden, seemingly out of the blue, you sit up, take stock, and realize your actual situation in life.

There you are, and you suddenly realize that you are spending your whole life just barely getting by. You keep up a good front. You manage to make ends meet somehow and look OK from the outside. But those periods of desperation, those times when you feel everything caving in on you, you keep those to yourself. You are a mess. And you know it. But you hide it beautifully. Meanwhile, way down under all that, you just know there has got to be some other way to live, some better way to look at the world, some way to touch life more fully. You click into it by chance now and then. You get a good job. You fall in love. You win the game. And for a while, things are different. Life takes on a richness and clarity that makes all the bad times and humdrum fade away. The whole texture of your experience changes and you say to yourself, "OK, now I've made it; now I will be happy." But then that fades, too, like smoke in the wind. You are left with just a memory. That and the vague awareness that something is wrong.

But there is really another whole realm of depth and sensitivity available in life, somehow, you are just not seeing it. You wind up feeling cut off. You feel insulated from the sweetness of experience by some sort of sensory cotton. You are not really touching life. You are not making it again. And then even that vague awareness fades away, and you are back to the same old reality. The world looks like the usual foul place, which is boring at best. It is an emotional roller coaster, and you spend a lot of your time down at the bottom of the ramp, yearning for the heights.

So what is wrong with you? Are you a freak? No. You are just human. And you suffer from the same malady that infects every human being. It is a monster inside all of us, and it has many arms: chronic tension, lack of genuine compassion for others, including the people closest to you, feelings being blocked up, and emotional deadness. Many, many arms. None of us is entirely free from it. We may deny it. We try to suppress it. We build a whole culture around hiding from it, pretending it is not there, and distracting ourselves from it with goals and projects and status. But it never goes away. It is a constant undercurrent in every thought and every perception; a little wordless voice at the back of the head that keeps saying, "Not good enough yet. Got to have more. Got to make it better. Got to be better." It is a monster, a monster that manifests everywhere in subtle forms.

Go to a party. Listen to the laughter, that brittle-tongued voice that says fun on the surface and fear underneath. Feel the tension, feel the pressure. Nobody really relaxes. They are faking it. Go to a ball game. Watch the fans in the stand. Watch the irrational fit of anger. Watch the uncontrolled frustration bubbling forth from people that masquerades under the guise of enthusiasm, or team spirit. Booing, cat-calls and unbridled egotism in the name of team loyalty. Drunkenness, fights in the stands. These are people trying desperately to release tension from within. These are not people who are at peace with themselves. Watch the news on TV. Listen to the lyrics in popular songs. You find the same theme repeated over and over in variations. Jealousy, suffering, discontent, and stress.

Life seems to be a perpetual struggle, some enormous effort against staggering odds. And what is our solution to all this dissatisfaction? We get stuck in the "if only" syndrome. If only I had more money, then I would be happy. If only I could find somebody who would really love me, if only I could lose 20 pounds, if only I had a color TV, a Jacuzzi, and curly hair, and on and on forever. So where does all this junk come from, and more important, what can we do about it? It comes from the conditions of our own minds. It is a deep, subtle, and pervasive set of mental habits, a Gordian knot which we have built up bit by bit and we can unravel just that same way, one piece at a time. We can tune up our awareness, dredge up each separate piece, and bring it out into the light. We can make the unconscious conscious, slowly, one piece at a time.

The essence of our experience is change. Change is incessant.

9

Moment by moment life flows by and it is never the same. Perpetual alteration is the essence of the perceptual universe. A thought springs up in your head and half a second later, it is gone. In comes another one, and that is gone too. A sound strikes your ears, and then silence. Open your eyes and the world pours in, blink and it is gone. People come into your life and they leave again. Friends go, relatives die. Your fortunes go up, and they go down. Sometimes you win and just as often you lose. It is incessant: change, change, change. No two moments ever the same.

There is not a thing wrong with this. It is the nature of the universe. But human culture has taught us some odd responses to this endless flowing. We categorize experiences. We try to stick each perception, every mental change in this endless flow, into one of three mental pigeon holes. It is good, or it is bad, or it is neutral. Then, according to which box we stick it in, we perceive with a set of fixed habitual mental responses. If a particular perception has been labeled "good," then we try to freeze time right there. We grab onto that particular thought, we fondle it, we hold it, and we try to keep it from escaping. When that does not work, we go all-out in an effort to repeat the experience which caused that thought. Let us call this mental habit "grasping."

Over on the other side of the mind lies the box labeled "bad." When we perceive something "bad," we try to push it away. We try to deny it, reject it, and get rid of it any way we can. We fight against our own experience. We run from pieces of ourselves. Let us call this mental habit "rejecting." Between these two reactions lies the neutral box. Here we place the experiences which are neither good nor bad. They are tepid, neutral, uninteresting, and boring. We pack experience away in the neutral box so that we can ignore it and thus return our attention to where the action is, namely our endless round of desire and aversion. This category of experience gets robbed of its fair share of our attention. Let us call this mental habit "ignoring." The direct result of all this lunacy is a perpetual treadmill race to nowhere, endlessly pounding after pleasure, endlessly fleeing from pain, endlessly ignoring 90 percent of our experience. Then wondering why life tastes so flat. In the final analysis, it's a system that does not work.

No matter how hard you pursue pleasure and success, there are times when you fail. No matter how fast you flee, there are times when pain catches up with you. And in between those times, life is so boring you could scream. Our minds are full of opinions and criticisms. We have built walls all around ourselves and are trapped in the prison of our own likes and dislikes. We suffer.

Suffering is a big word in Buddhist thought. It is a key term and it should be thoroughly understood. The Pali word is *dukkha,* and it does not just mean the agony of the body. It means that deep, subtle sense of unsatisfactoriness which is a part of every mind moment and which results directly from the mental treadmill. The essence of life is suffering, said the Buddha. At first glance this seems exceedingly morbid and pessimistic. It even seems untrue. After all, there are plenty of times when we are happy. Aren't there? No, there are not. It just seems that way. Take any moment when you feel really fulfilled and examine it closely. Down under the joy, you will find that subtle, all-pervasive undercurrent of tension, that no matter how great this moment is, it is going to end. No matter how much you just gained, you are either going to lose some of it or spend the rest of your days guarding what you have got and scheming how to get more. And in the end, you are going to die. In the end, you lose everything. It is all transitory. Sounds pretty bleak, doesn't it? Luckily it's not; not at all. It only sounds bleak when you view it from the level of ordinary mental perspective, the very level at which the treadmill mechanism operates. Down under that level lies another perspective, a completely different way to look at the universe. It is a level of functioning where the mind does not try to freeze time, where we do not grasp onto our experience as it flows by, where we do not try to block things out and ignore them. It is a level of experience beyond good and bad, beyond pleasure and pain. It is a lovely way to perceive the world, and it is a learnable skill. It is not easy, but it can be learned.

Happiness and peace. Those are really the prime issues in human existence. That is what all of us are seeking. This often is a bit hard to see because we cover up those basic goals with layers of surface objectives. We want food, we want money, we want sex, possessions, and respect. We even say to ourselves that the idea of "happiness" is too abstract: "Look, I am practical. Just give me enough money and I will buy all the happiness I need." Unfortunately, this is an attitude that does not work. Examine each of these goals and you will find they are superficial. You want food. Why? Because I am hungry. So you are hungry, so what? Well, if I eat, I won't be hungry, and then I'll feel good. Ah ha! Feel good! Now there is the real item. What we really seek is not the surface goals. They are just means to an end. What we are really after is that feeling of relief that comes when the drive is satisfied. Relief, relaxation, and an end to the tension. Peace, happiness, no more yearning.

So what is this happiness? For most of us, the perfect happiness would mean getting everything we wanted, being in control of everything, playing Caesar, making the whole world dance a jig according to our every whim. Once again, it does not work that way. Take a look at the people in history who have actually held this type of power. These were not happy people. Most assuredly they were not men at peace with themselves. Why? Because they were driven to control the world totally and absolutely and they could not. They wanted to control all men, yet there remained men who refused to be controlled. They could not control the stars. They still got sick. They still had to die.

You can't ever get everything you want. It is impossible. Luckily, there is another option. You can learn to control your mind, to step outside of this endless cycle of desire and aversion. You can learn not to want what you want, to recognize desires but not be controlled by them. This does not mean that you lie down on the road and invite everybody to walk all over you. It means that you continue to live a very normal-looking life, but live from a whole new viewpoint. You do the things that a person must do, but you are free from that obsessive, compulsive drivenness of your own desires. You want something, but you don't need to chase after it. You fear something, but you don't need to stand there quaking in your boots. This sort of mental culture is very difficult. It takes years. But trying to control everything is impossible, and the difficult is preferable to the impossible.

Wait a minute, though. Peace and happiness! Isn't that what civilization is all about? We build skyscrapers and freeways. We have paid vacations, TV sets. We provide free hospitals and sick leaves, Social Security and welfare benefits. All of that is aimed at providing some measure of peace and happiness. Yet the rate of mental illness climbs steadily, and

13

the crime rates rise faster. The streets are crawling with aggressive and unstable individuals. Stick your arms outside the safety of your own door and somebody is very likely to steal your watch! Something is not working. A happy man does not steal. A man at peace with himself does not feel driven to kill. We like to think that our society is exploiting every area of human knowledge in order to achieve peace and happiness.

We are just beginning to realize that we have overdeveloped the material aspect of existence at the expense of the deeper emotional and spiritual aspect, and we are paying the price for that error. It is one thing to talk about degeneration of moral and spiritual fiber in America today, and another thing to do something about it. The place to start is within ourselves. Look carefully inside, truly and objectively, and each of us will see moments when "I am the punk" and "I am the crazy." We will learn to see those moments, see them clearly, cleanly and without condemnation, and we will be on our way up and out of being so.

You can't make radical changes in the pattern of your life until you begin to see yourself exactly as you are now. As soon as you do that, changes flow naturally. You don't have to force or struggle or obey rules dictated to you by some authority. You just change. It is automatic. But arriving at that initial insight is quite a task. You've got to see who you are and how you are, without illusion, judgment, or resistance of any kind. You've got to see your own place in society and your function as a social being. You've got to see your duties and obligations to your fellow human beings, and above all, your responsibility to yourself as an individual living with other individuals. And you've got to see all of that clearly and as a unit, a single gestalt of interrelationship. It sounds complex, but it often occurs in a single instant. Mental culture through meditation is without rival in helping you achieve this sort of understanding and serene happiness.

The *Dhammapada* is an ancient Buddhist text which anticipated Freud by thousands of years. It says: "What you are now is the result of what you were. What you will be tomorrow will be the result of what you are now. The consequences of an evil mind will follow you like the cart follows the ox that pulls it. The consequences of a purified mind will follow you like your own shadow. No one can do more for you than your own purified mind—no parent, no relative, no friend, no one. A well-disciplined mind brings happiness."

Meditation is intended to purify the mind. It cleanses the thought process of what can be called psychic irritants, things like greed, hatred, and jealousy, things that keep you snarled up in emotional bondage. It brings the mind to a state of tranquility and awareness, a state of concentration and insight.

In our society, we are great believers in education. We believe that knowledge makes a cultured person civilized. Civilization, however, polishes the person superficially. Subject our noble and sophisticated gentleman to the stresses of war or economic collapse, and see what happens. It is one thing to obey the law because you know the penalties and fear the consequences. It is something else entirely to obey the law because you have cleansed yourself from the greed that would make you steal and the hatred that would make you kill. Throw a stone into a stream. The running water would smooth the surface, but the inner part remains unchanged. Take that same stone and place it in the intense

15

fires of a forge, and the whole stone changes inside and outside. It all melts. Civilization changes man on the outside. Meditation softens him within, through and through. Meditation is called the Great Teacher. It is the cleansing crucible fire that works slowly through understanding. The greater your understanding, the more flexible and tolerant you can be. The greater your understanding, the more compassionate you can be. You become like a perfect parent or an ideal teacher. You are ready to forgive and forget. You feel love toward others because you understand them. And you understand others because you have understood yourself. You have looked deeply inside and seen self-illusion and your own human failings. You have seen your own humanity and learned to forgive and to love. When you have learned compassion for yourself, compassion for others is automatic. An accomplished meditator has achieved a profound understanding of life, and he inevitably relates to the world with a deep and uncritical love.

Meditation is a lot like cultivating a new land. To make a field out of a forest, first you have to clear the trees and pull out the stumps. Then you till the soil and you fertilize it. Then you sow your seed and you harvest your crops. To cultivate your mind, first you have to clear out the various irritants that are in the way, pull them right out by the root so that they won't grow back. Then you fertilize. You pump energy and discipline into the mental soil. Then you sow the seed and you harvest your crops of faith, morality, mindfulness, and wisdom.

Faith and morality, by the way, have a special meaning in this context. Buddhism does not advocate faith in the sense of believing something because it is written in a book or attributed to a prophet or taught to you by some authority figure. The meaning here is closer to confidence. It is knowing that something is true because you have seen it work, because you have observed that very thing within yourself. In the same way, morality is not a ritualistic obedience to some exterior, imposed code of behavior. It is rather a healthy habit pattern which you have consciously and voluntarily chosen to impose upon yourself because you recognize its superiority to your present behavior.

The purpose of meditation is personal transformation. The you that goes in one side of the meditation experience is not the same you that comes out the other side. It changes your character by a process of sensitization, by making you deeply aware of your own thoughts, words, and deeds. Your arrogance evaporates and your antagonism dries up. Your mind becomes still and calm. And your life smoothes out. Thus meditation properly performed prepares you to meet the ups and downs of existence. It reduces your tension, your fear, and your worry. Restlessness recedes, and passion moderates. Things begin to fall into place and your life becomes a glide instead of a struggle. All of this happens through understanding.

Meditation sharpens your concentration and your thinking power. Then, piece by piece, your own subconscious motives and mechanics become clear to you. Your intuition sharpens. The precision of your thought increases and gradually you come to a direct knowledge of things as they really are, without prejudice and without illusion. So is this reason enough to bother? Scarcely. These are just promises on paper. There is only one way you will ever know if meditation is worth the effort. Learn to do it right, and do it. See for yourself.

CHAPTER 2

# WHAT MEDITATION ISN'T

M editation is a word. You have heard this word before
or you would never have picked up this book. The
thinking process operates by association, and all sorts of
ideas are associated with the word "meditation." Some of
them are probably accurate, and others are hogwash. Some
of them pertain more properly to other systems of meditation and have nothing to do with Vipassana practice. Before
we proceed, it behooves us to blast some of that residue out
of our own neuronal circuits so that new information can pass
unimpeded. Let us start with some of the most obvious stuff.

We are not going to teach you to contemplate your navel
or to chant secret syllables. You are not conquering demons
or harnessing invisible energies. There are no colored belts
given for your performance, and you don't have to shave
your head or wear a turban. You don't even have to give
away all your belongings and move to a monastery. In fact,
unless your life is immoral and chaotic, you can probably
get started right away and make some sort of progress.
Sounds fairly encouraging, wouldn't you say?

There are many, many books on the subject of meditation.
Most of them are written from a point of view which lies
squarely within one particular religious or philosophical
tradition, and many of the authors have not bothered to
point this out. They make statements about meditation
which sound like general laws, but are actually highly specific
procedures exclusive to that particular system of practice.

19

The result is something of a muddle. Worse yet is the panoply of complex theories and interpretations available, all of them at odds with one another. The result is a real mess and an enormous jumble of conflicting opinions accompanied by a mass of extraneous data. This book is specific. We are dealing exclusively with the Vipassana system of meditation. We are going to teach you to watch the functioning of your own mind in a calm and detached manner so you can gain insight into your own behavior. The goal is awareness, an awareness so intense, concentrated, and finely tuned that you will be able to pierce the inner workings of reality itself.

There are a number of common misconceptions about meditation. We see them crop up again and again from new students, the same questions over and over. It is best to deal with these things at once, because they are the sort of preconceptions which can block your progress right from the outset. We are going to take these misconceptions one at a time and dissolve them.

MISCONCEPTION 1—*Meditation is just a relaxation technique.*

The bugaboo here is the word *just*. Relaxation is a key component of meditation, but Vipassana-style meditation aims at a much loftier goal. Nevertheless, the statement is essentially true for many other systems of meditation. All meditation procedures stress concentration of the mind, bringing the mind to rest on one item or one area of thought. Do it strongly and thoroughly enough, and you achieve a deep and blissful relaxation which is called *Jhana*. It is a state of such supreme tranquility that it amounts to rapture. It is a form of pleasure which lies above and beyond anything that can be experienced in the normal state of consciousness. Most systems stop right there. That is the goal, and when you attain that, you simply repeat the experience for the rest of your life. Not so with Vipassana meditation. Vipassana seeks another goal—awareness. Concentration and relaxation are considered necessary concomitants to awareness. They are required precursors, handy tools, and beneficial by-products. But they are not the goal. The goal is insight. Vipassana meditation is a profound religious practice aimed at nothing less than the purification and transformation of your everyday life. We will deal more thoroughly with the differences between concentration and insight in Chapter 14.

MISCONCEPTION 2—*Meditation means going into a trance.*

Here again the statement could be applied accurately to certain systems of meditation, but not to Vipassana. Insight meditation is not a form of hypnosis. You are not trying to black out your mind so as to become unconscious. You are not trying to turn yourself into an emotionless vegetable. If anything, the reverse is true. You will become more and more attuned to your own emotional changes. You will learn to know yourself with ever greater clarity and precision. In learning this technique, certain states do occur which may appear trancelike to the observer. But they are really quite the opposite. In hypnotic trance, the subject is susceptible to control by another party, whereas in deep concentration the meditator remains very much under his own control. The similarity is superficial, and in any case, the occurrence of these phenomena is not the point of Vipassana. As we have said, the deep concentration of *Jhana* is a tool or stepping stone on the route of heightened awareness. Vipassana by definition is the cultivation of mindfulness or awareness. If you find that you are becoming

21

unconscious in meditation, then you aren't meditating, according to the definition of that word as used in the Vipassana system. It is that simple.

MISCONCEPTION 3—*Meditation is a mysterious practice which cannot be understood.*

Here again, this is almost true, but not quite. Meditation deals with levels of consciousness which lie deeper than symbolic thought. Therefore, some of the data about meditation just won't fit into words. That does not mean, however, that it cannot be understood. There are deeper ways to understand things than by the use of words. You understand how to walk. You probably can't describe the exact order in which your nerve fibers and your muscles contract during that process. But you can do it. Meditation needs to be understood that same way, by doing it. It is not something that you can learn in abstract terms. It is not something to be talked about. It is something to be experienced. Meditation is not a mindless formula which gives automatic and predictable results. You can never really predict exactly what will come up during any particular session. It is an investigation and an experiment; an adventure every time. In fact, this is so true that when you do reach a feeling of predictability and sameness in your practice, you use that as an indicator. It means that you have gotten off the track somewhere and you are headed for stagnation. Learning to look at each second as if it were the first and only second in the universe is most essential in Vipassana meditation.

MISCONCEPTION 4—*The purpose of meditation is to become a psychic superbeing.*

No, the purpose of meditation is to develop awareness.

Learning to read minds is not the point. Levitation is not the goal. The goal is liberation. There is a link between psychic phenomena and meditation, but the relationship is somewhat complex. During early stages of the meditator's career, such phenomena may or may not arise. Some people may experience some intuitive understanding or memories from past lives; others do not. In any case, these are not regarded as well-developed and reliable psychic abilities. Nor should they be given undue importance. Such phenomena are in fact fairly dangerous to new meditators in that they are quite seductive. They can be an ego trap which can lure you right off the track. Your best approach is not to place any emphasis on these phenomena. If they come up, that's fine. If they don't, that's fine, too. There is a point in the meditator's career where he may practice special exercises to develop psychic powers. But this occurs way down the line. After he has gained a very deep stage of *Jhana*, the meditator will be far enough advanced to work with such powers without the danger of their running out of control or taking over his life. He will then develop them strictly for the purpose of service to others. This state of affairs occurs in most cases only after decades of practice. Don't worry about it. Just concentrate on developing more and more awareness. If voices and visions pop up, just notice them and let them go. Don't get involved.

MISCONCEPTION 5—*Meditation is dangerous, and a prudent person should avoid it.*

Everything is dangerous. Walk across the street and you may get hit by a bus. Take a shower and you could break your neck. Meditate and you will probably dredge up various nasty matters from your past. The suppressed material that has been buried there for quite some time can be scary. It is also highly profitable. No activity is entirely without risk, but that does not mean that we should wrap ourselves in some protective cocoon. That is not living. That is premature death. The way to deal with danger is to know approximately how much of it there is, where it is likely to be found and how to deal with it when it arises. That is the purpose of this manual. Vipassana is development of awareness. That in itself is not dangerous; on the contrary, increased awareness is the safeguard against danger. Properly done, meditation is a very gentle and gradual process. Take it slow and easy, and the development of your practice will occur very naturally. Nothing should be forced. Later, when you are under the close scrutiny and protective wisdom of a competent teacher, you can accelerate your rate of growth by taking a period of intensive meditation. In the beginning, though, easy does it. Work gently and everything will be fine.

MISCONCEPTION 6—*Meditation is for saints and holy men, not for regular people.*

You find this attitude very prevalent in Asia, where monks and holy men are accorded an enormous amount of ritualized reverence. This is somewhat akin to the American attitude of idolizing movie stars and baseball heroes. Such people are stereotyped, made larger than life, and saddled with all sorts of characteristics that few human beings can ever live up to. Even in the West, we share some of this attitude about meditation. We expect the meditator to be some extraordinarily pious figure in whose mouth butter would never dare to melt. A little personal contact with such people will quickly dispel this illusion. They usually prove to be people of enormous energy and gusto, people who live their lives with amazing vigor. It is true, of course, that most holy men meditate, but they don't meditate because they are holy men. That is backward. They are holy men because they meditate. Meditation is how they got there. And they started meditating before they became holy, otherwise they would not be holy. This is an important point. A sizable number of students seems to feel that a person should be completely moral before he begins meditation. It is an unworkable strategy. Morality requires a certain degree of mental control. It's a prerequisite. You can't follow any set of moral precepts without at least a little self-control, and if your mind is perpetually spinning like a fruit cylinder in a one-armed bandit, self-control is highly unlikely. So mental culture has to come first.

There are three integral factors in Buddhist meditation— morality, concentration, and wisdom. Those three factors grow together as your practice deepens. Each one influences the other, so you cultivate the three of them together, not one at a time. When you have the wisdom to truly understand a situation, compassion towards all the parties involved is automatic, and compassion means that you automatically restrain yourself from any thought, word, or deed that might harm yourself or others. Thus your behavior is automatically moral. It is only when you don't understand things deeply that you create problems. If you fail to see the consequences of your own action, you will blunder. The fellow who waits to become totally moral before he begins to meditate is waiting for a "but" that will never come. The ancient sages say that he is like a man waiting for the ocean to become calm so that he can go take a bath.

To understand this relationship more fully, let us propose

that there are levels of morality. The lowest level is adherence to a set of rules and regulations laid down by somebody else. It could be your favorite prophet. It could be the state, the head man of your tribe, or your father. No matter who generates the rules, all you've got to do at this level is know the rules and follow them. A robot can do that. Even a trained chimpanzee could do it if the rules were simple enough and he was smacked with a stick every time he broke one. This level requires no meditation at all. All you need are the rules and somebody to swing the stick.

The next level of morality consists of obeying the same rules even in the absence of somebody who will smack you. You obey because you have internalized the rules. You smack yourself every time you break one. This level requires a bit of mind control. If your thought pattern is chaotic, your behavior will be chaotic, too. Mental culture reduces mental chaos.

There is a third level of morality, but it might be better termed ethics. This level is a whole quantum leap up the scale, a real paradigm shift in orientation. At the level of ethics, a person does not follow hard and fast rules dictated by authority. A person chooses to follow a path dictated by mindfulness, wisdom and compassion. This level requires real intelligence and an ability to juggle all the factors in every situation to arrive at a unique, creative, and appropriate response each time. Furthermore, the individual making these decisions needs to have dug himself out of his own limited personal viewpoint. He has to see the entire situation from an objective point of view, giving equal weight to his own needs and those of others. In other words, he has to be free from greed, hatred, envy, and all the other selfish junk that ordinarily keeps us from seeing the other guy's side of the issue.

Only then can he choose that precise set of actions which will be truly optimal for that situation. This level of morality absolutely demands meditation, unless you were born a saint. There is no other way to acquire the skill. Furthermore, the sorting process required at this level is exhausting. If you tried to juggle all those factors in every situation with your conscious mind, you'd wear yourself out. The intellect just can't keep that many balls in the air at once. It is an overload. Luckily, a deeper level of consciousness can do this sort of processing with ease. Meditation can accomplish the sorting process for you. It is an eerie feeling.

One day you've got a problem—let's say, to handle Uncle Herman's latest divorce. It looks absolutely unsolvable, an enormous muddle of "maybes" that would give Solomon himself the willies. The next day you are washing the dishes, thinking about something else entirely, and suddenly the solution is there. It just pops out of the deep mind and you say, "Ah ha!" and the whole thing is solved. This sort of intuition can only occur when you disengage the logic circuits from the problem and give the deep mind the opportunity to cook up the solution. The conscious mind just gets in the way. Meditation teaches you how to disentangle yourself from the thought process. It is the mental art of stepping out of your own way, and that's a pretty useful skill in everyday life. Meditation is certainly not an irrelevant practice strictly for ascetics and hermits. It is a practical skill that focuses on everyday events and has immediate application in everybody's life. Meditation is not other-worldly.

Unfortunately, this very fact constitutes the drawback for certain students. They enter the practice expecting instantaneous cosmic revelation, complete with angelic choirs. What they usually get is a more efficient way to take out the trash and better ways to deal with Uncle Herman. They are needlessly disappointed. The trash solution comes first. The voices of archangels take a bit longer.

MISCONCEPTION 7—*Meditation is running away from reality.*

Incorrect. Meditation is running into reality. It does not insulate you from the pain of life. It allows you to delve so deeply into life and all its aspects that you pierce the pain barrier and go beyond suffering. Vipassana is a practice done with the specific intention of facing reality, to fully experience life just as it is and to cope with exactly what you find. It allows you to blow aside the illusions and free yourself from all those polite little lies you tell yourself all the time. What is there is there. You are who you are, and lying to yourself about your own weaknesses and motivations only binds you tighter on to the wheel of illusion. Vipassana meditation is not an attempt to forget yourself or to cover up your troubles. It is learning to look at yourself exactly as you are. See what is there, accept it fully. Only then can you change it.

MISCONCEPTION 8—*Meditation is a great way to get high.*

Well, yes and no. Meditation does produce lovely blissful feelings sometimes. But they are not the purpose, and they don't always occur. Furthermore, if you do meditation with that purpose in mind, they are less likely to occur than if you just meditate for the actual purpose of meditation, which is increased awareness. Bliss results from relaxation, and relaxation results from release of tension. Seeking bliss from meditation introduces tension into the process, which blows the whole chain of events. It is a Catch-22. You can only have bliss if you don't chase it. Besides, if euphoria and good feelings are what you are after, there are easier ways to get them. They are available in taverns and from shady characters on street corners all across the nation. Euphoria is not the purpose of meditation. It will often arise, but it is to be regarded as a by-product. Still, it is a very pleasant side effect, and it becomes more and more frequent the longer you meditate. You won't hear any disagreement about this from advanced practitioners.

MISCONCEPTION 9—*Meditation is selfish.*

It certainly looks that way. There sits the meditator parked on his little cushion. Is he out giving blood? No. Is he busy working with disaster victims? No. But let us examine his motivation. Why is he doing this? His intention is to purge his own mind of anger, prejudice, and ill-will. He is actively engaged in the process of getting rid of greed, tension, and insensitivity. Those are the very items which obstruct his compassion for others. Until they are gone, any good works that he does are likely to be just an extension of his own ego and of no real help in the long run. Harm in the name of help is one of the oldest games. The grand inquisitor of the Spanish Inquisition spouted the loftiest of motives. The Salem witchcraft trials were conducted for the "public good." Examine the personal lives of advanced meditators and you will often find them engaged in humanitarian service. You will seldom find them as crusading missionaries who are willing to sacrifice certain individuals for the sake of some pious idea. The fact is we are more selfish than we know. The ego has a way of turning the loftiest activities into trash if it is allowed free range. Through meditation we become aware of ourselves exactly as we are, by waking up to the numerous subtle ways that we manifest our own selfishness. Then we truly begin to be genuinely selfless. Cleansing yourself of selfishness is not a selfish activity.

MISCONCEPTION 10—*When you meditate, you sit around thinking lofty thoughts.*

Wrong again. There are certain systems of contemplation in which this sort of thing is done. But that is not Vipassana. Vipassana is the practice of awareness. Awareness of whatever is there, be it supreme truth or crummy trash. What is there, is there. Of course, lofty aesthetic thoughts may arise during your practice. They are certainly not to be avoided. Neither are they to be sought. They are just pleasant side effects. Vipassana is a simple practice. It consists of experiencing your own life events directly, without preference and without mental images pasted to them. Vipassana is seeing your life unfold from moment to moment without biases. What comes up, comes up. It is very simple.

MISCONCEPTION 11—*A couple of weeks of meditation and all my problems will go away.*

Sorry, meditation is not a quick cure-all. You will start seeing changes right away, but really profound effects are years down the line. That is just the way the universe is constructed. Nothing worthwhile is achieved overnight. Meditation is tough in some respects. It requires a long discipline and sometimes a painful process of practice. At each sitting you gain some results, but those results are often very subtle. They occur deep within the mind, only to manifest much later. And if you are sitting there constantly looking for some huge instantaneous changes, you will miss the subtle shifts altogether. You will get discouraged, give up and swear that no such changes will ever occur. Patience is the key. Patience. If you learn nothing else from meditation, you will learn patience. And that is the most valuable lesson available.

CHAPTER 3

# WHAT MEDITATION IS

Meditation is a word, and words are used in different ways by different speakers. This may seem like a trivial point, but it is not. It is quite important to distinguish exactly what a particular speaker means by the words he uses. Every culture on earth, for example, has produced some sort of mental practice which might be termed meditation. It all depends on how loose a definition you give to that word. Everybody does it, from Africans to Eskimos. The techniques are enormously varied, and we will make no attempt to survey them. There are other books for that. For the purpose of this volume, we will restrict our discussion to those practices best known to Western audiences and most likely associated with the term meditation.

Within the Judeo-Christian tradition we find two overlapping practices called prayer and contemplation. Prayer is a direct address to a spiritual entity. Contemplation is a prolonged period of conscious thought about a specific topic, usually a religious ideal or scriptural passage. From the standpoint of mental culture, both of these activities are exercises in concentration. The normal deluge of conscious thought is restricted, and the mind is brought to one conscious area of operation. The results are those you find in any concentrative practice: deep calm, a physiological slowing of the metabolism and a sense of peace and well-being.

Out of the Hindu tradition comes Yogic meditation, which is also purely concentrative. The traditional basic exercises consist of focusing the mind on a single object—a stone, a candle flame, a syllable or whatever, and not allowing it to wander. Having acquired the basic skill, the yogi proceeds to expand his practice by taking on more complex objects of meditation chants, colorful religious images, energy channels in the body and so forth. Still, no matter how complex the object of meditation, the meditation itself remains purely an exercise in concentration.

Within the Buddhist tradition, concentration is also highly valued. But a new element is added and more highly stressed. That element is awareness. All Buddhist meditation aims at the development of awareness, using concentration as a tool. The Buddhist tradition is very wide, however, and there are several diverse routes to this goal. Zen meditation uses two separate tacks. The first is the direct plunge into awareness by sheer force of will. You sit down and you just sit, meaning that you toss out of your mind everything except pure awareness of sitting. This sounds very simple. It is not. A brief trial will demonstrate just how difficult it really is. The second Zen approach used in the Rinzai school is that of tricking the mind out of conscious thought and into pure awareness. This is done by giving a student an unsolvable riddle which he must solve anyway, and by placing him in a horrendous training situation. Since he cannot flee from the pain of the situation, he must flee into a pure experience of the moment. There is nowhere else to go. Zen is tough. It is effective for many people, but it is really tough.

Another strategem, Tantric Buddhism, is nearly the reverse. Conscious thought, at least the way we usually do it, is the manifestation of ego, the you that you usually think that you are. Conscious thought is tightly connected with self-concept. The self-concept or ego is nothing more than a set of reactions and mental images which are artificially pasted to the flowing process of pure awareness. Tantra seeks to obtain pure awareness by destroying this ego image. This is accomplished by a process of visualization. The student is given a particular religious image to meditate upon, for example, one of the deities from the Tantric pantheon. He does this in so thorough a fashion that he becomes that entity. He takes off his own identity and puts on another. This takes a while, as you might imagine, but it works. During the process, he is able to watch the way that the ego is constructed and put in place. He comes to recognize the arbitrary nature of all egos, including his own, and he escapes from bondage to the ego. He is left in a state where he may have an ego if he so chooses, either his own or whichever other he might wish, or he can do without one. Result: pure awareness. Tantra is not exactly a game of patty cake either.

Vipassana is the oldest of Buddhist meditation practices. The method comes directly from the *Satipatthana Sutta,* a discourse attributed to the Buddha himself. Vipassana is a direct and gradual cultivation of mindfulness or awareness. It proceeds piece by piece over a period of years. The student's attention is carefully directed to an intense examination of certain aspects of his own existence. The meditator is trained to notice more and more of his own flowing life experience. Vipassana is a gentle technique. But it also is very, very thorough. It is an ancient and codified system of training your mind, a set of exercises dedicated to becoming more and more aware of your own life experience. It is attentive listening, mindful seeing and careful testing. We learn to smell acutely, to touch fully, and really pay attention to the changes taking place in all these experiences. We learn to listen to our own thoughts without being caught up in them.

The object of Vipassana practice is to learn to see the truth of impermanence, unsatisfactoriness, and selflessness of phenomena. We think we are doing this already, but that is an illusion. It comes from the fact that we are paying so little attention to the ongoing surge of our own life experiences that we might just as well be asleep. We are simply not paying enough attention to notice that we are not paying attention. It is another Catch-22.

Through the process of mindfulness, we slowly become aware of what we really are down below the ego image. We wake up to what life really is. It is not just a parade of ups and downs, lollipops and smacks on the wrist. That is an illusion. Life has a much deeper texture than that if we bother to look, and if we look in the right way.

Vipassana is a form of mental training that will teach you to experience the world in an entirely new way. You will learn for the first time what is truly happening to you, around you and within you. It is a process of self discovery, a participatory investigation in which you observe your own experiences while participating in them as they occur. The practice must be approached with this attitude: "Never mind what I have been taught. Forget about theories and prejudices and stereotypes. I want to understand the true nature of life. I want to know what this experience of being alive really is. I want to apprehend the true and deepest qualities of life, and I don't want to just accept somebody else's explanation. I want to see it for myself."

If you pursue your meditation practice with this attitude, you will succeed. You'll find yourself observing things objectively, exactly as they are—flowing and changing from moment to moment. Life then takes on an unbelievable richness which cannot be described. It has to be experienced.

The Pali term for Insight meditation is *Vipassana Bhavana*. *Bhavana* comes from the root *bhu*, which means to grow or to become. Therefore *Bhavana* means to cultivate, and the word is always used in reference to the mind. *Bhavana* means mental cultivation. *Vipassana* is derived from two roots. *Passana* means seeing or perceiving. *Vi* is a prefix with a complex set of connotations. The basic meaning is "in a special way." But there also is the connotation of both "into" and "through." The whole meaning of the word is looking into something with clarity and precision, seeing each component as distinct, and piercing all the way through so as to perceive the most fundamental reality of that thing. This process leads to insight into the basic reality of whatever is being inspected. Put it all together and *Vipassana Bhavana* means the cultivation of the mind, aimed at seeing in the special way that leads to insight and to full understanding.

In Vipassana meditation we cultivate this special way of seeing life. We train ourselves to see reality exactly as it is, and we call this special mode of perception *mindfulness*. This process of mindfulness is really quite different from what we usually do. We usually do not look into what is really there in front of us. We see life through a screen of thoughts and concepts, and we mistake those mental objects for the reality. We get so caught up in this endless thought-stream that reality flows by unnoticed. We spend our time engrossed in activity, caught up in an eternal pursuit of pleasure and gratification and an eternal flight from pain and unpleasantness. We spend all of our energies trying to make ourselves feel better, trying to bury our fears. We are endlessly seeking security. Meanwhile, the world of real experience flows by untouched and untasted. In Vipassana meditation we train ourselves to ignore the constant impulses to be more comfortable, and we dive into the reality instead. The ironic thing is that real peace comes only when you stop chasing it. Another Catch-22.

When you relax your driving desire for comfort, real fulfillment arises. When you drop your hectic pursuit of gratification, the real beauty of life comes out. When you seek to know the reality without illusion, complete with all its pain and danger, that is when real freedom and security are yours. This is not another doctrine we are trying to drill into you. This is an observable reality, a thing you can and should see for yourself.

Buddhism is 2,500 years old, and any thought system of that vintage has time to develop layers and layers of doctrine and ritual. Nevertheless, the fundamental attitude of Buddhism is intensely empirical and anti-authoritarian. Gotama the Buddha was a highly unorthodox individual and real anti-traditionalist. He did not offer his teaching as a set of dogmas, but rather as a set of propositions for each individual to investigate for himself. His invitation to one and all was "Come and see." One of the things he said to his followers was, "Place no head above your own." By this he meant, don't accept somebody else's word. See for yourself.

We want you to apply this attitude to every word you read in this manual. We are not making statements that you should accept merely because we are authorities in the field. Blind faith has nothing to do with this. These are experiential realities. Learn to adjust your mode of perception according to instructions given in the book, and you will see for yourself. That and only that provides ground for your faith. Insight meditation is essentially a practice of investigative personal discovery.

Having said this, we will present here a very short synopsis of some of the key points of Buddhist philosophy. We make no attempt to be thorough, since that has been quite nicely done in many other books. This material is essential to understanding Vipassana, therefore, some mention must be made.

From the Buddhist point of view, we human beings live in a very peculiar fashion. We view impermanent things as permanent, though everything is changing all around us. The process of change is constant and eternal. As you read these words, your body is aging. But you pay no attention to that. The book in your hand is decaying. The print is fading and the pages are becoming brittle. The walls around you are aging. The molecules within those walls are vibrating at an enormous rate, and everything is shifting, going to pieces and dissolving slowly. You pay no attention to that, either. Then one day you look around you. Your body is wrinkled and squeaky and you hurt. The book is a yellowed, useless lump; the building is caving in. So you pine for lost youth and you cry when the possessions are gone. Where does this pain come from? It comes from your own inattention. You failed to look closely at life. You failed to observe the constantly shifting flow of the world as it went by. You set up the collection of mental constructions, "me," "the book," "the building," and you assumed that those were solid, real entities. You assumed that they would endure forever. They never do. But you can tune into the constant change. You can learn to perceive your life as an ever-flowing movement. You can learn to see the continuous flow of all conditioned things. You can learn this. It is just a matter of time and training.

Our human perceptual habits are remarkably stupid in some ways. We tune out 99 percent of all the sensory stimuli we actually receive, and we solidify the remainder into discrete mental objects. Then we react to those mental objects in programmed habitual ways.

An example: There you are, sitting alone in the stillness of a peaceful night. A dog barks in the distance, which, in itself, is neither good nor bad in itself. Up out of that sea of silence come surging waves of sonic vibration. You start to hear the lovely complex patters, and they are turned into scintillating electronic stimulations within the nervous system. The process should be used as an experience of impermanence, unsatisfactoriness and selflessness. We humans tend to ignore it totally. Instead, we solidify that perception into a mental object. We paste a mental picture on it and we launch into a series of emotional and conceptual reactions to it. "There is that dog again. He is always barking at night. What a nuisance. Every night he is a real bother. Somebody should do something. Maybe I should call a cop. No, a dog catcher. I'll call the pound. No, maybe I'll just write a real nasty letter to the guy who owns that dog. No, too much trouble. I'll just get an ear plug." These are just perceptual and mental habits. You learn to respond this way as a child by copying the perceptual habits of those around you. These perceptual responses are not inherent in the structure of the nervous system. The circuits are there. But this is not the only way that our mental machinery can be used. That which has been learned can be unlearned. The first step is to realize what you are doing, as you are doing it, to stand back and quietly watch.

From the Buddhist perspective, we humans have a backward view of life. We look at what is actually the cause of suffering and we see it as happiness. The cause of suffering is that desire-aversion syndrome which we spoke of earlier. Up pops a perception. It could be anything—a beautiful girl, a handsome guy, a speedboat, a thug with a gun, a truck bearing down on you, anything. Whatever it is, the very next thing we do is to react to the stimulus with a feeling about it.

Take worry. We worry a lot. Worry itself is the problem. Worry is a process. It has steps. Anxiety is not just a state of existence but a procedure. What you've got to do is to look at the very beginning of that procedure, those initial stages before the process has built up a head of steam. The very first link of the worry chain is the grasping-rejecting reaction. As soon as a phenomenon pops into the mind, we try mentally to grab onto it or push it away. That sets the worry response in motion. Luckily, there is a handy little tool called Vipassana meditation which you can use to short-circuit the whole mechanism.

Vipassana meditation teaches us how to scrutinize our own perceptual process with great precision. We learn to watch the arising of thought and perception with a feeling of serene detachment. We learn to view our own reactions to stimuli with calm and clarity. We begin to see ourselves reacting without getting caught up in the reactions themselves. The obsessive nature of thought slowly dies. We can still get married. We can still step out of the path of the truck. But we don't need to go through hell over either one.

This escape from the obsessive nature of thought produces a whole new view of reality. It is a complete paradigm shift, a total change in the perceptual mechanism. It brings with it the bliss of emancipation from obsessions. Because of these advantages, Buddhism views this way of looking at things as a correct view of life and Buddhist texts call it seeing things as they really are.

Vipassana meditation is a set of training procedures which open us gradually to this new view of reality as it truly is. Along with this new reality goes a new view of that most central aspect of reality: "me." A close inspection reveals that we have done the same thing to "me" that we have done to all other perceptions. We have taken a flowing vortex of thought, feeling and sensation and we have solidified that into a mental construct. Then we have stuck a label onto it: "me." And forever after, we treat it as if it were a static and enduring entity. We view it as a thing separate from all other things. We pinch ourselves off from the rest of that process of eternal change which is the universe. And then we grieve over how lonely we feel. We ignore our inherent connectedness to all other beings and we decide that "I" have to get more for "me;" then we marvel at how greedy and insensitive human beings are. And on it goes. Every evil deed, every example of heartlessness in the world stems directly from this false sense of "me" as distinct from all else that is out there.

Explode the illusion of that one concept and your whole universe changes. Don't expect to do this overnight, however. You spent your whole life building up that concept, reinforcing it with every thought, word, and deed over all those years. It is not going to evaporate instantly. But it will pass if you give it enough time and enough attention. Vipassana meditation is a process by which it is dissolved. Little by little, you chip away at it just by watching it.

The "I" concept is a process. It is a thing we are doing. In Vipassana we learn to see that we are doing it, when we are doing it, and how we are doing it. Then it moves and fades away, like a cloud passing through a clear sky. We are left in a state where we can do it or not do it, whichever seems appropriate to the situation. The compulsiveness is gone. We have a choice.

These are all major insights, of course. Each one is a deep-reaching understanding of one of the fundamental issues of human existence. They do not occur quickly, nor without considerable effort. But the payoff is big. They lead to a total transformation of your life. Every second of your existence thereafter is changed. The meditator who pushes all the way down this track achieves perfect mental health, a pure love for all that lives and complete cessation of suffering. That is no small goal. But you don't have to go all the way to reap benefits. They start right away and they pile up over the years. It is a cumulative function. The more you sit, the more you learn about the real nature of your own existence. The more hours you spend in meditation, the greater your ability to calmly observe every impulse and intention, every thought and emotion just as it arises in the mind. Your progress to liberation is measured in cushion man-hours. And you can stop any time you've had enough. There is no stick over your head except your own desire to see the true quality of life, to enhance your own existence and that of others.

Vipassana meditation is inherently experiential. It is not theoretical. In the practice of meditation you become sensitive to the actual experience of living, to how things feel. You do not sit around developing subtle and aesthetic thoughts about living. You live. Vipassana meditation more than anything else is learning to live.

# CHAPTER 4

## ATTITUDE

Within the last century, Western science and physics have made a startling discovery. We are part of the world we view. The very process of our observation changes the things we observe. As an example, an electron is an extremely tiny item. It cannot be viewed without instrumentation, and that apparatus dictates what the observer will see. If you look at an electron in one way, it appears to be a particle, a hard little ball that bounces around in nice straight paths. When you view it another way, an electron appears to be a wave form, with nothing solid about it. It glows and wiggles all over the place. An electron is an event more than a thing. And the observer participates in that event by the very process of his or her observation. There is no way to avoid this interaction.

Eastern science has recognized this basic principle for a very long time. The mind is a set of events, and the observer participates in those events every time he or she looks inward. Meditation is participatory observation. What you are looking at responds to the process of looking. What you are looking at is you, and what you see depends on how you look. Thus, the process of meditation is extremely delicate, and the result depends absolutely on the state of mind of the meditator. The following attitudes are essential to success in practice. Most of them have been presented before. But we bring them together again here as a series of rules for application.

*1) Don't expect anything:* Just sit back and see what happens. Treat the whole thing as an experiment. Take an active interest in the test itself. But don't get distracted by your expectations about the results. For that matter, don't be anxious for any result whatsoever. Let the meditation move along at its own speed and in its own direction. Let the meditation teach you what it wants you to learn. Meditative awareness seeks to see reality exactly as it is. Whether that corresponds to our expectations or not, it requires a temporary suspension of all our preconceptions and ideas. We must store away our images, opinions, and interpretations out of the way for the duration of the session. Otherwise we will stumble over them.

*2) Don't strain:* Don't force anything or make grand exaggerated efforts. Meditation is not aggressive. There is no violent striving. Just let your effort be relaxed and steady.

*3) Don't rush:* There is no hurry, so take your time. Settle yourself on a cushion, and sit as though you have the whole day. Anything really valuable takes time to develop. Patience, patience, patience.

*4) Don't cling to anything and don't reject anything:* Let come what comes, and accommodate yourself to that, whatever it is. If good mental images arise, that is fine. If bad mental images arise, that is fine, too. Look on all of it as equal, and make yourself comfortable with whatever happens. Don't fight with what you experience, just observe it all mindfully.

*5) Let go:* Learn to flow with all the changes that come up. Loosen up and relax.

*6) Accept everything that arises:* Accept your feelings, even the ones you wish you did not have. Accept your experiences, even the ones you hate. Don't condemn yourself for having human flaws and failings. Learn to see all the phenomena in the mind as being perfectly natural and understandable. Try to exercise a disinterested acceptance at all times and with respect to everything you experience.

7) *Be gentle with yourself:* Be kind to yourself. You may not be perfect, but you are all you've got to work with. The process of becoming who you will be begins first with the total acceptance of who you are.

8) *Investigate yourself:* Question everything. Take nothing for granted. Don't believe anything because it sounds wise and pious and some holy men said it. See for yourself. That does not mean that you should be cynical, impudent, or irreverent. It means you should be empirical. Subject all statements to the actual test of your own experience and let the results be your guide to truth. Insight meditation evolves out of an inner longing to wake up to what is real and to gain liberating insight into the true structure of existence. The entire practice hinges upon this desire to be awake to the truth. Without it, the practice is superficial.

9) *View all problems as challenges:* Look upon negatives that arise as opportunities to learn and to grow. Don't run from them, condemn yourself, or bury your burden in saintly silence. You have a problem? Great. More grist for the mill. Rejoice, dive in, and investigate.

10) *Don't ponder:* You don't need to figure everything out. Discursive thinking won't free you from the trap. In meditation, the mind is purified naturally by mindfulness, by wordless bare attention. Habitual deliberation is not necessary to eliminate those things that are keeping you in bondage. All that is necessary is a clear, non-conceptual perception of

what they are and how they work. That alone is sufficient to dissolve them. Concepts and reasoning just get in the way. Don't think. See.

*11) Don't dwell upon contrasts:* Differences do exist between people, but dwelling upon them is a dangerous process. Unless carefully handled, it leads directly to egotism. Ordinary human thinking is full of greed, jealousy, and pride. A man seeing another man on the street may immediately think, "He is better looking than I am." The instant result is envy or shame. A girl seeing another girl may think, "I am prettier than she is." The instant result is pride. This sort of comparison is a mental habit, and it leads directly to ill feeling of one sort or another: greed, envy, pride, jealousy, hatred. It is an unskillful mental state, but we do it all the time. We compare our looks with others, our success, our accomplishments, our wealth, possessions, or I.Q. and all these lead to the same state—estrangement, barriers between people, and ill feeling.

The meditator's job is to cancel this unskillful habit by examining it thoroughly, and then replacing it with another. Rather than noticing the differences between self and others, the meditator trains himself to notice similarities. He centers his attention on those factors that are universal to all life, things that will move him closer to others. Thus his comparison, if any, leads to feelings of kinship rather than feelings of estrangement.

Breathing is a universal process. All vertebrates breathe in essentially the same manner. All living things exchange gases with their environment in some way or other. This is one of the reasons that breathing is chosen as the focus of meditation. The meditator is advised to explore the process of his own breathing as a vehicle for realizing his own inherent connectedness with the rest of life. This does not mean that we shut our eyes to all the differences around us. Differences exist. It means simply that we de-emphasize contrasts and emphasize the universal factors that we have in common. The recommended procedure is as follows: When we as meditators perceive any sensory object, we are not to dwell upon it in the ordinary egotistical way. We should rather examine the very process of perception itself. We should watch what that object does to our senses and our perception. We should watch the feelings that arise and the mental activities that follow. We should note the changes that occur in our own consciousness as a result. In watching all these phenomena, we must be aware of the universality of what we are seeing. That initial perception will spark pleasant, unpleasant or neutral feelings. That is a universal phenomenon. It occurs in the minds of others just as it does in our own, and we should see that clearly. By following these feelings various reactions may arise. We may feel greed, lust, or jealousy. We may feel fear, worry, restlessness, or boredom. These reactions are universal. We simply note them and then generalize. We should realize that these reactions are normal human responses and can arise in anybody.

The practice of this style of comparison may feel forced and artificial at first, but it is no less natural than what we ordinarily do. It is merely unfamiliar. With practice, this habit pattern replaces our normal habit of egoistic comparing and feels far more natural in the long run. We become very understanding people as a result. We no longer get upset by the "failings" of others. We progress toward harmony with all life.

# CHAPTER 5

## THE PRACTICE

Although there are many subjects of meditation, we strongly recommend you start with focusing your total undivided attention on your breathing to gain some degree of shallow concentration. Remember that you are not practicing a deep absorption or pure concentration technique. You are practicing mindfulness for which you need only a certain degree of shallow concentration. You want to cultivate mindfulness culminating in insight and wisdom to realize the truth as it is. You want to know the working of your body-mind complex exactly as it is. You want to get rid of all psychological annoyance to make your life really peaceful and happy.

The mind cannot be purified without seeing things as they really are. "Seeing things as they really are" is such a heavily loaded and ambiguous phrase. Many beginning meditators wonder what we mean, for anyone who has clear eyesight can see objects as they are.

When we use this phrase in reference to insight gained from our meditation, what we mean is not seeing things superficially with our regular eyes, but seeing things with wisdom as they are in themselves. Seeing with wisdom means seeing things within the framework of our body-mind complex without prejudices or biases springing from our greed, hatred, and delusion. Ordinarily when we watch the working of our body-mind complex, we tend to hide or ignore things which are not pleasant to us and to hold onto

51

things which are pleasant. This is because our minds are generally influenced by desire, resentment, and delusion. Our ego, self, or opinions get in our way and color our judgment.

When we mindfully watch our bodily sensations, we should not confuse them with mental formations, for bodily sensation can arise without anything to do with the mind. For instance, we sit comfortably. After a while, there can arise some uncomfortable feeling on our back or in our legs. Our mind immediately experiences that discomfort and forms numerous thoughts around the feeling. At that point, without trying to confuse the feeling with the mental formations, we should isolate the feeling as feeling and watch it mindfully. Feeling is one of the seven universal mental factors. The other six are contact, perception, attention, concentration, life force, and volition.

At another time, we may have a certain emotion, such as resentment, fear, or lust. Then we should watch the emotion exactly as it is without trying to confuse it with anything else. When we bundle our form, feeling, perceptions, mental formations, and consciousness into one and try to watch all of them as feeling, we get confused, as we will not be able to see the source of feeling. If we simply dwell upon the feeling alone, ignoring other mental factors, our realization of truth becomes very difficult.

We want to gain the insight into the experience of impermanence to overcome our resentment; our deeper knowledge of unhappiness overcomes our greed which causes our unhappiness; our realization of selflessness overcomes ignorance arising from the notion of self. We should first see the mind and body as separate. Having comprehended them separately, we should see their essential interconnectedness.

As our insight becomes sharpened, we become more and more aware of the fact that all the aggregates are cooperating to work together. None can exist without the other. We can see the real meaning of the famous metaphor of the blind man who has a healthy body to walk and the disabled person who has very good eyes to see. Neither of them alone can do much for himself. But when the disabled person climbs on the shoulders of the blind man, together they can travel and achieve their goals easily. Similarly, the body alone can do nothing for itself. It is like a log unable to move or do anything by itself except to become a subject of impermanence, decay and death. The mind itself can do nothing without the support of the body. When we mindfully watch both body and mind, we can see how many wonderful things they do together.

As long as we are sitting in one place we may gain some degree of mindfulness. Going to a retreat and spending several days or several months watching our feelings, perceptions, countless thoughts, and various states of consciousness may make us eventually calm and peaceful. Normally we do not have that much time to spend in one place meditating all the time. Therefore, we should find a way to apply our mindfulness to our daily life in order for us to be able to handle daily unforeseeable eventualities.

What we face every day is unpredictable. Things happen due to multiple causes and conditions, as we are living in a conditional and impermanent world. Mindfulness is our emergency kit, readily available at our service at any time. When we face a situation in which we feel indignation, if we mindfully investigate our own mind, we will discover bitter truths about ourselves. For example, that we are selfish; we are egocentric; we are attached to our ego; we hold on to our opinions; we think we are right and everybody else is wrong; we are prejudiced; we are biased; and at the bottom of all of this, we do not really love ourselves. This discovery, though bitter, is a most rewarding experience. And in the long run, this discovery delivers us from deeply rooted psychological and spiritual suffering.

Mindfulness practice is the practice of being 100 percent honest with ourselves. When we watch our own mind and body, we notice certain things that are unpleasant to realize. As we do not like them, we try to reject them. What are the things we do not like? We do not like to detach ourselves from loved ones or to live with unloved ones. We include not only people, places, and material things into our likes and dislikes, but opinions, ideas, beliefs, and decisions as well. We do not like what naturally happens to us. We do not like, for instance, growing old, becoming sick, becoming weak, or showing our age, for we have a great desire to preserve our appearance. We do not like someone pointing out our faults, for we take great pride in ourselves. We do not like someone to be wiser than we are, for we are deluded about ourselves. These are but a few examples of our personal experience of greed, hatred, and ignorance.

When greed, hatred, and ignorance reveal themselves in our daily lives, we use our mindfulness to track them down and comprehend their roots. The root of each of these mental states is within ourselves. If we do not, for instance, have the root of hatred, nobody can make us angry, for it is the root of our anger that reacts to somebody's actions or words or behavior. If we are mindful, we will diligently use our wisdom to look into our own mind. If we do not have hatred in us we will not be concerned when someone points out our shortcomings. Rather, we will be thankful to the person who draws our attention to our faults. We have to be extremely wise and mindful to thank the person who explicates our faults so we will be able to tread the upward path toward improving ourselves. We all have blind spots. The other person is our mirror for us to see our faults with wisdom. We should consider the person who shows our shortcomings as one who excavates a hidden treasure in us that we were unaware of. It is by knowing the existence of our deficiencies that we can improve ourselves. Improving ourselves is the unswerving path to the perfection which is our goal in life. Only by overcoming weaknesses can we cultivate noble qualities hidden deep down in our subconscious mind. Before we try to surmount our defects, we should know what they are.

If we are sick, we must find out the cause of our sickness. Only then can we get treatment. If we pretend that we do not have sickness even though we are suffering, we will never get treatment. Similarly, if we think that we don't have these faults, we will never clear our spiritual path. If we are blind to our own flaws, we need someone to point them out to us. When they point out our faults, we should be grateful to them like the Venerable Sariputta, who said: "Even if a seven-year-old novice monk points out my mistakes, I will accept them with utmost respect for him." Venerable Sariputta was an Arahant who was 100 percent mindful and had no fault in him. But since he did not have any pride, he was able to maintain this position. Although we are not Arahants, we should determine to emulate his example, for our goal in life also is to attain what he attained.

Of course, the person pointing out our mistakes himself may not be totally free from defects, but he can see our problems as we can see his faults, which he does not notice until we point them out to him. Pointing out shortcomings and responding to them should both be done mindfully. If someone becomes unmindful in indicating faults and uses unkind and harsh language, he might do more harm than good to himself as well as to the person whose shortcomings he points out. One who speaks with resentment cannot be mindful and is unable to express himself clearly. One who feels hurt while listening to harsh language may lose his mindfulness and not hear what the other person is really saying. We should speak mindfully and listen mindfully to be benefited by talking and listening. When we listen and talk mindfully, our minds are free from greed, selfishness, hatred and delusion.

OUR GOAL

As meditators, we all must have a goal, for if we do not have a goal, we will simply be groping in the dark blindly following somebody's instructions on meditation. There must certainly be a goal for whatever we do consciously and willingly. It is not the Vipassana meditator's goal to become enlightened before other people or to have more power or to make more profit than others. Meditators are not in competition with each other for mindfulness.

Our goal is to reach the perfection of all the noble and wholesome qualities latent in our subconscious mind. This goal has five elements to it: purification of mind, overcoming sorrow and lamentation, overcoming pain and grief, treading the right path leading to attainment of eternal peace, and attaining happiness by following that path. Keeping this fivefold goal in mind, we can advance with hope and confidence to reach the goal.

PRACTICE

Once you sit, do not change the position again until the end of the time you determined at the beginning. Suppose you change your original position because it is uncomfortable, and assume another position. What happens after a while is that the new position becomes uncomfortable. Then you want another and after a while it, too, becomes uncomfortable. So you may go on shifting, moving, changing one position to another the whole time you are on your meditation cushion and you may not gain a deep and meaningful level of concentration. Therefore, you must make every effort not to change your original position. We will discuss how to deal with pain in Chapter 10.

To avoid changing your position, determine at the beginning of meditation how long you are going to meditate. If you have never meditated before, sit motionlessly for not longer than twenty minutes. As you repeat your practice, you can increase your sitting time. The length of sitting depends on how much time you have for sitting meditation practice and how long you can sit without excruciating pain.

We should not have a time schedule to attain the goal, for our attainment depends on how we progress in our practice based on our understanding and development of our spiritual faculties. We must work diligently and mindfully towards the goal without setting any particular time schedule to reach it. When we are ready, we get there. All we have to do is to prepare ourselves for that attainment.

After sitting motionlessly, close your eyes. Our mind is analogous to a cup of muddy water. The longer you keep a cup of muddy water still, the more the mud settles down and the water will be seen clearly. Similarly, if you keep quiet without moving your body, focusing your entire undivided attention on the subject of your meditation, your mind settles down and begins to experience the bliss of meditation.

To prepare for this attainment, we should keep our mind in the present moment. The present moment is changing so fast that a casual observer does not seem to notice its existence at all. Every moment is a moment of events and no moment passes by without an event. We cannot notice a moment without noticing events taking place in that moment. Therefore, the moment we try to pay bare attention to is the present moment. Our mind goes through a series of events like a series of pictures passing through a projector. Some of these pictures are coming from our past experiences and others are our imaginations of things that we plan to do in the future.

The mind can never be focused without a mental object. Therefore we must give our mind an object which is readily available every present moment. One such object is our breath. The mind does not have to make a great effort to find the breath. Every moment the breath is flowing in and out through our nostrils. As our practice of insight meditation is taking place every waking moment, our mind finds it very easy to focus itself on the breath, for it is more conspicuous and constant than any other object.

After sitting in the manner explained earlier and having shared your loving-kindness with everybody, take three deep breaths. After taking three deep breaths, breathe normally, letting your breath flow in and out freely, effortlessly, and begin focusing your attention on the rims of your nostrils. Simply notice the feeling of breath going in and out. When one inhalation is complete and before exhaling begins, there is a brief pause. Notice it and notice the beginning of exhaling. When the exhalation is complete, there is another brief pause before inhaling begins. Notice this brief pause, too. This means that there are two brief pauses of breath—one at the end of inhaling and the other at the end of exhaling. These two pauses occur in such a brief moment you may not be aware of their occurrence. But when you are mindful, you can notice them.

Do not verbalize or conceptualize anything. Simply notice the incoming and outgoing breath without saying, "I breathe in," or "I breathe out." When you focus your attention on the breath ignore any thought, memory, sound, smell, taste, etc., and focus your attention exclusively on the breath, nothing else.

At the beginning, both the inhalations and exhalations are short because the body and mind are not calm and relaxed. Notice the feeling of that short inhaling and short exhaling as they occur without saying, "short inhaling," or "short exhaling." As you continue to notice the feeling of short inhaling and short exhaling, your body and mind become relatively calm. Then your breath becomes long. Notice the feeling of that long breath as it is without saying, "Long breath." Then notice the entire breathing process from the beginning to the end. Subsequently the breath becomes subtle, and the mind and body become calmer than before. Notice this calm and peaceful feeling of your breathing.

## WHAT TO DO WHEN THE MIND WANDERS AWAY

In spite of your concerted effort to keep the mind on your breathing, the mind may wander away. It may go to past experiences and suddenly you may find yourself remembering places you've visited, people you met, friends not seen for a long time, a book you read long ago, the taste of food you ate yesterday, and so on. As soon as you notice that your mind is no longer on your breath, mindfully bring it back and anchor it there. However, in a few moments you may be caught up again thinking how to pay your bills, to make a telephone call to your friend, write a letter to someone, do your laundry, buy your groceries, go to a party, plan your next vacation, and so forth. As soon as you notice that your mind is not on your object, bring it back mindfully. Following are some suggestions to help you gain the concentration necessary for the practice of mindfulness.

### 1. Counting

In a situation like this, counting may help. The purpose of counting is simply to focus the mind on the breath. Once your mind is focused on the breath, give up counting. This is a device for gaining concentration. There are numerous ways of counting. Any counting should be done mentally. Do not make any sound when you count. Following are some of the ways of counting.

*a)* While breathing in, count "one, one, one, one..." until the lungs are full of fresh air. While breathing out count "two, two, two, two..." until the lungs are empty of fresh air. Then while breathing in again count "three, three, three, three, three..." until the lungs are full again and while breathing out count again "four, four, four, four..." until the lungs are empty of fresh air. Count up to ten and repeat as many times as necessary to keep the mind focused on the breath.

*b)* The second method of counting is counting rapidly up to ten. While counting "one, two, three, four, five, six, seven, eight, nine and ten," breathe in, and again while counting "one, two, three, four, five, six, seven, eight, nine and ten," breathe out. This means that with one inhalation you should count up to ten and with one exhalation you should count up to ten. Repeat this way of counting as many times as necessary to focus the mind on the breath.

*c)* The third method of counting is to count in succession up to ten. At this time, count "one, two, three, four, five" (only up to five) while inhaling and then count "one, two, three, four, five, six" (up to six) while exhaling. Again, count "one, two, three, four, five, six, seven" (only up to seven) while inhaling. Then count "one, two, three, four, five, six, seven, eight" while exhaling. Count up to nine while inhaling and count up to ten while exhaling. Repeat this way of counting as many times as necessary to focus the mind on the breath.

*d)* The fourth method is to take a long breath. When the lungs are full, mentally count "one" and breathe out completely until the lungs are empty of fresh air. Then count mentally "two." Take a long breath again and count "three" and breathe out completely as before. When the lungs are empty of fresh air, count mentally "four." Count your breath in this manner up to ten. Then count backward from ten to one. Count again from one to ten and then ten to one.

*e)* The fifth method is to join inhaling and exhaling. When the lungs are empty of fresh air, count mentally "one." This time you should count both inhalation and exhalation as one. Again inhale, exhale, and mentally count "two." This way of counting should be done only up to five and repeated from five to one. Repeat this method until your breathing becomes refined and quiet.

Remember that you are not supposed to continue your counting all the time. As soon as your mind is locked at the nostril-tip where the inhalation and exhalation touch and you begin to feel that your breathing is so refined and quiet that you cannot notice inhalation and exhalation separately, you should give up counting. Counting is used only to train the mind to concentrate on one object.

## 2. Connecting

After inhaling do not wait to notice the brief pause before exhaling but connect the inhaling with exhaling, so you can notice both inhaling and exhaling as one continuous breath.

## 3. Fixing

After joining inhaling with exhaling, fix your mind on the point where you feel your inhaling and exhaling breath touching. Inhale and exhale as one single breath moving in and out touching or rubbing the rims of your nostrils.

## 4. Focus your mind like a carpenter

A carpenter draws a straight line on a board that he wants to cut. Then he cuts the board with his saw along the straight line he drew. He does not look at the teeth of his saw as they move in and out of the board. Rather he focuses his entire attention on the line he drew so he can cut the board straight. Similarly, keep your mind straight on the point where you feel the breath at the rims of your nostrils.

## 5. Make your mind like a gatekeeper

A gatekeeper does not take into account any detail of the people entering a house. All he does is notice people entering the house and leaving the house through the gate. Similarly, when you concentrate you should not take into account any detail of your experiences. Simply notice the feeling of your inhaling and exhaling breath as it goes in and out right at the rims of your nostrils.

As you continue your practice your mind and body become so light that you may feel as if you are floating in the air or on water. You may even feel that your body is springing up into the sky. When the grossness of your in-and-out breathing has ceased, subtle in-and-out breathing arises. This very subtle breath is your mind's object of focus. This is the sign of concentration. This first appearance of a sign-object will be replaced by a more and more subtle sign-object. This subtlety of the sign can be compared to the sound of a bell. When a bell is struck with a big iron rod, you hear a gross sound at first. As the sound fades away, the sound becomes very subtle. Similarly, the in-and-out breath appears at first as a gross sign. As you keep paying bare attention to it, this sign becomes very subtle. But the consciousness remains totally focused on the rims of the nostrils. Other meditation objects become clearer and clearer, as the sign develops. But the breath becomes subtler and subtler as the sign develops. Because of this subtlety, you may not notice the presence of your breath. Don't get disappointed thinking that you lost your breath or that nothing is happening to your meditation practice. Don't worry. Be mindful and determined to bring your feeling of breath back to the rims of your nostrils. This is the time you should practice more vigorously, balancing your energy, faith, mindfulness, concentration, and wisdom.

## FARMER'S SIMILE

Suppose there is a farmer who uses buffaloes for plowing his rice field. As he is tired in the middle of the day, he unfastens his buffaloes and takes a rest under the cool shade of a tree. When he wakes up, he does not find his animals. He does not worry, but simply walks to the water place where all the animals gather for drinking in the hot midday and he finds his buffaloes there. Without any problem he brings them back and ties them to the yoke again and starts plowing his field.

Similarly, as you continue this exercise, your breath becomes so subtle and refined that you might not be able to notice the feeling of breath at all. When this happens do not worry. It has not disappeared. It is still where it was before—right at the nostril-tips. Take a few quick breaths and you will notice the feeling of breathing again. Continue to pay bare attention to the feeling of the touch of breath at the rims of your nostrils.

As you keep your mind focused on the rims of your nostrils, you will be able to notice the sign of the development of meditation. You will feel the pleasant sensation of a sign. Different meditators experience this differently. It will be like a star, or a round gem, or a round pearl, or a cotton seed, or a peg made of heartwood, or a long string, or a wreath of flowers, or a puff of smoke, or a cobweb, or a film of cloud, or a lotus flower, or the disc of the moon, or the disc of the sun.

Earlier in your practice you had inhaling and exhaling as objects of meditation. Now you have the sign as the third object of meditation. When you focus your mind on this third object, your mind reaches a stage of concentration sufficient for your practice of insight meditation. This sign is strongly present at the rims of the nostrils. Master it and gain full control of it so that whenever you want, it should be available. Unite the mind with this sign which is available in the present moment and let the mind flow with every succeeding moment. As you pay bare attention to it, you will see that the sign itself is changing every moment. Keep your mind with the changing moments. Also, notice that your mind can be concentrated only on the present moment. This unity of the mind with the present moment is called momentary concentration. As moments are incessantly passing away one after another, the mind keeps pace with them, changing with them, appearing and disappearing with them without clinging to any of them. If we try to stop the mind at one moment, we end up in frustration because the mind cannot be held fast. It must keep up with what is happening in the new moment. As the present moment can be found any moment, every waking moment can be made a concentrated moment.

To unite the mind with the present moment, we must find something happening in that moment. However, you cannot focus your mind on every changing moment without a certain degree of concentration to keep pace with the moment. Once you gain this degree of concentration, you can use it for focusing your attention on anything you experience—the rising and falling of your abdomen, the rising and falling of the chest area, the rising and falling of any feeling, or the rising and falling of your breath or thoughts and so on.

To make any progress in insight meditation you need this kind of momentary concentration. That is all you need for the insight meditation practice because everything in your experience lives only for one moment. When you focus this concentrated state of mind on the changes taking place in your mind and body, you will notice that your breath is the physical part and the feeling of breath, consciousness of the feeling, and the consciousness of the sign are the mental parts. As you notice them you can notice that they are

changing all the time. You may have various types of sensations, other than the feeling of breathing, taking place in your
body. Watch them all over your body. Don't try to create any
feeling which is not naturally present in any part of your
body. But notice whatever sensation arises in the body.
When thought arises notice it, too. All you should notice
in all these occurrences is the impermanent, unsatisfactory,
and selfless nature of all your experiences whether mental
or physical.

As your mindfulness develops, your resentment for the
change, your dislike for the unpleasant experiences, your
greed for the pleasant experiences, and the notion of selfhood
will be replaced by the deeper awareness of impermanence,
unsatisfactoriness, and selflessness. This knowledge of reality
in your experience helps you to foster a more calm, peaceful, and mature attitude toward your life. You will see what
you thought in the past to be permanent is changing with
such inconceivable rapidity that even your mind cannot
keep up with these changes. Somehow you will be able to
notice many of the changes. You will see the subtlety of
impermanence and the subtlety of selflessness. This insight
will show you the way to peace, happiness, and will give
you the wisdom to handle your daily problems in life.

When the mind is united with the breath flowing all the
time, we will naturally be able to focus the mind on the present moment. We can notice the feeling arising from contact of breath with the rim of our nostrils. As the earth element of the air that we breathe in and out touches the earth
element of our nostrils, the mind feels the flow of air in and
out. The warm feeling arises at the nostrils or any other part
of the body from the contact of the heat element generated
by the breathing process. The feeling of impermanence of

breath arises when the earth element of flowing breath touches the nostrils. Although the water element is present in the breath, the mind cannot feel it.

Also, we feel the expansion and contraction of our lungs, abdomen, and lower abdomen, as the fresh air is pumped in and out of the lungs. The expansion and contraction of the abdomen, lower abdomen, and chest are parts of the universal rhythm. Everything in the universe has the same rhythm of expansion and contraction just like our breath and body. All of them are rising and falling. However, our primary concern is the rising and falling phenomena of the breath and minute parts of our minds and bodies.

Along with the inhaling breath, we experience a small degree of calmness. This little degree of calmness turns into tension if we don't breathe out in a few moments. As we breathe out this tension is released. After breathing out, we experience discomfort if we wait too long before having fresh air brought in again. This means that every time our lungs are full we must breathe out and every time our lungs are empty we must breathe in. As we breathe in, we experience a small degree of calmness, and as we breathe out, we experience a small degree of calmness. We desire calmness and relief of tension and do not like the tension and feeling resulting from the lack of breath. We wish that the calmness would stay longer and the tension disappear more quickly than it normally does. But the tension will not go away as fast as we wish nor will the calmness stay as long as we wish. And again we get agitated or irritated, for we desire the calmness to return and stay longer and the tension to go away quickly and not to return again. Here we see how even a small degree of desire for permanency in an impermanent situation causes pain or unhappiness. Since there is no self-entity to control this situation, we will become more disappointed.

However, if we watch our breathing without desiring calmness and without resenting the tension arising from breathing in and out, and experience only the impermanence, the unsatisfactoriness, and selflessness of our breath, our mind becomes peaceful and calm.

The mind does not stay all the time with the feeling of breath. It goes to sounds, memories, emotions, perceptions, consciousness, and mental formations as well. When we experience these states, we should forget about the feeling of breath and immediately focus our attention on these states—one at a time, not all of them at one time. As they fade away, we let our mind return to the breath which is the home base the mind can return to from quick or long journeys to various states of mind and body. We must remember that all these mental journeys are made within the mind itself.

Every time the mind returns to the breath, it comes back with a deeper insight into impermanence, unsatisfactoriness, and selflessness. The mind becomes more insightful from the impartial and unbiased watching of these occurrences. The mind gains insight into the fact that this body, these feelings, the various states of consciousness and numerous mental formations are to be used only for the purpose of gaining deeper insight into the reality of this body-mind complex.

# Chapter 6

# What To Do With Your Body

The practice of meditation has been going on for several thousand years. That is quite a bit of time for experimentation, and the procedure has been very, very thoroughly refined. Buddhist practice has always recognized that the mind and body are tightly linked and that each influences the other. Thus, there are certain recommended physical practices which will greatly help you to master this skill. And these practices should be followed. Keep in mind, however, that these postures are practice aids. Don't confuse the two. Meditation does not mean sitting in the lotus position. It is a mental skill. It can be practiced anywhere you wish. But these postures will help you to learn this skill and they speed your progress and development. So use them.

## General Rules

The purpose of the various postures is threefold. First, they provide a stable feeling in the body. This allows you to remove your attention from such issues as balance and muscular fatigue, so that you can center your concentration on the formal object of meditation. Second, they promote physical immobility which is then reflected by an immobility of mind. This creates a deeply settled and tranquil concentration. Third, they give you the ability to sit for a long period of time without yielding to the meditator's three main enemies—pain, muscular tension, and falling asleep.

The most essential thing is to sit with your back straight.

69

The spine should be erect with the spinal vertebrae held like a stack of coins, one on top of the other. Your head should be held in line with the rest of the spine. All of this is done in a relaxed manner. No stiffness. You are not a wooden soldier, and there is no drill sergeant. There should be no muscular tension involved in keeping the back straight. Sit light and easy. The spine should be like a firm young tree growing out of soft ground. The rest of the body just hangs from it in a loose, relaxed manner. This is going to require a bit of experimentation on your part. We generally sit in tight, guarded postures when we are walking or talking and in sprawling postures when we are relaxing. Neither of those will do. But they are cultural habits and they can be relearned.

Your objective is to achieve a posture in which you can sit for the entire session without moving at all. In the beginning, you will probably feel a bit odd to sit with a straight back. But you will get used to it. It takes practice, and an erect posture is very important. This is what is known in physiology as a position of arousal, and with it goes mental alertness. If you slouch, you are inviting drowsiness. What you sit on is equally important. You are going to need a chair or a cushion, depending on the posture you choose, and the firmness of the seat must be chosen with some care. Too soft a seat can put you right to sleep. Too hard can promote pain.

CLOTHING

The clothes you wear for meditation should be loose and soft. If they restrict blood flow or put pressure on nerves, the result will be pain and/or that tingling numbness which we normally refer to as our "legs going to sleep." If you are

70

wearing a belt, loosen it. Don't wear tight pants or pants made of thick material. Long skirts are a good choice for women. Loose pants made of thin or elastic material are fine for anybody. Soft, flowing robes are the traditional garb in Asia and they come in an enormous variety of styles such as sarongs and kimonos. Take your shoes off, and if your stockings are tight and binding, take them off, too.

## TRADITIONAL POSTURES

When you are sitting on the floor in the traditional Asian manner, you need a cushion to elevate your spine. Choose one that is relatively firm and at least three inches thick when compressed. Sit close to the front edge of the cushion and let your crossed legs rest on the floor in front of you. If the floor is carpeted, that may be enough to protect your shins and ankles from pressure. If it is not, you will probably need some sort of padding for your legs. A folded blanket will do nicely. Don't sit all the way back on the cushion. This position causes its front edge to press into the underside of your thigh, causing nerves to pinch. The result will be leg pain.

There are a number of ways you can fold your legs. We will list four in ascending order of preference.

*a) American Indian style.* Your right foot is tucked under the left knee and left foot is tucked under your right knee.

*b) Burmese style.* Both of your legs lie flat on the floor from knee to foot. They are parallel with each other and one in front of the other.

*c) Half lotus.* Both of your knees touch the floor. One leg and foot lie flat along the calf of the other leg.

*d) Full lotus.* Both knees touch the floor, and your legs are crossed at the calf. Your left foot rests on the right thigh, and your right foot rests on the left thigh. Both soles turn upward.

In all these postures, your hands are cupped one on the other, and they rest on your lap with the palms turned upward. The hands lie just below the navel with the bend of each wrist pressed against the thigh. This arm position provides firm bracing for the upper body. Don't tighten your neck or shoulder muscles. Relax your arms. Your diaphragm is held relaxed, expanded to maximum fullness. Don't let tension build up in the stomach area. Your chin is up. Your eyes can be open or closed. If you keep them open, fix them on the tip of your nose or in a middle distance straight in front. You are not looking at anything. You are just putting your eyes where there is nothing in particular to see, so that you can forget about vision. Don't strain, don't stiffen, and don't be rigid. Relax; let the body be natural and supple. Let it hang from the erect spine like a rag doll.

Half and full lotus positions are the traditional meditation postures in Asia. And the full lotus is considered the best. It is the most solid by far. Once you are locked into this position, you can be completely immovable for a very long period. Since it requires a considerable flexibility in the legs, not everybody can do it. Besides, the main criterion by which you choose a posture for yourself is not what others say about it. It is your own comfort. Choose a position that allows you to sit the longest without pain, without moving. Experiment with different postures. The tendons will loosen with practice. And then you can work gradually toward the full lotus.

## USING A CHAIR

Sitting on the floor may not be feasible for you because of pain or some other reason. No problem. You can always use a chair instead. Pick one that has a level seat, a straight back and no arms. It is best to sit in such a way that your back does not lean against the back of the chair. The furniture of the seat should not dig into the underside of your thighs. Place your legs side by side, feet flat on the floor. As with the traditional postures, place both hands on your lap, cupped one upon the other. Don't tighten your neck or shoulder muscles, and relax your arms. Your eyes can be open or closed.

In all the above postures, remember your objectives. You want to achieve a state of complete physical stillness, yet you don't want to fall asleep. Recall the analogy of the muddy water. You want to promote a totally settled state of the body which will engender a corresponding mental settling. There must also be a state of physical alertness which can induce the kind of mental clarity you seek. So experiment. Your body is a tool for creating desired mental states. Use it judiciously.

CHAPTER 7

# WHAT TO DO WITH YOUR MIND

The meditation we teach is called Insight meditation. As we have already said, the variety of possible objects of meditation is nearly unlimited, and human beings have used an enormous number down through the ages. Even within the Vipassana tradition there are variations. There are meditation teachers who teach their students to follow the breath by watching the rise and fall of the abdomen. Others recommend focusing attention on the touch of the body against the cushion, or hand against hand, or the feeling of one leg against the other. The method we are explaining here, however, is considered the most traditional and is probably what Gotama Buddha taught his students. The *Satipatthana Sutta,* the Buddha's original discourse on mindfulness, specifically says that one must begin by focusing the attention on the breathing and then go on to note all other physical and mental phenomena which arise.

We sit, watching the air going in and out of our noses. At first glance, this seems an exceedingly odd and useless procedure. Before going on to specific instructions, let us examine the reason behind it. The first question we might have is why use any focus of attention at all? We are, after all, trying to develop awareness. Why not just sit down and be aware of whatever happens to be present in the mind? In fact, there are meditations of that nature. They are sometimes referred to as unstructured meditation and they are quite difficult. The mind is tricky. Thought is an inherently

75

complicated procedure. By that we mean that we become trapped, wrapped up, and stuck in the thought chain. One thought leads to another which leads to another, and another, and another, and so on. Fifteen minutes later we suddenly wake up and realize we spent that whole time stuck in a daydream or sexual fantasy or a set of worries about our bills or whatever.

There is a difference between being aware of a thought and thinking a thought. That difference is very subtle. It is primarily a matter of feeling or texture. A thought you are simply aware of with bare attention feels light in texture; there is a sense of distance between that thought and the awareness viewing it. It arises lightly like a bubble, and it passes away without necessarily giving rise to the next thought in that chain. Normal conscious thought is much heavier in texture. It is ponderous, commanding, and compulsive. It sucks you in and grabs control of consciousness. By its very nature it is obsessional, and it leads straight to the next thought in the chain, with apparently no gap between them.

Conscious thought sets up a corresponding tension in the body, such as muscular contraction or a quickening of the heartbeat. But you won't feel tension until it grows to actual pain, because normal conscious thought is also greedy. It grabs all your attention and leaves none to notice its own effect. The difference between being aware of the thought and thinking the thought is very real. But it is extremely subtle and difficult to see. Concentration is one of the tools needed to be able to see this difference.

Deep concentration has the effect of slowing down the thought process and speeding up the awareness viewing it. The result is the enhanced ability to examine the thought process. Concentration is our microscope for viewing subtle internal states. We use the focus of attention to achieve one-pointedness of mind with calm and constantly applied attention. Without a fixed reference point you get lost, overcome by the ceaseless waves of change flowing round and round within the mind.

We use breath as our focus. It serves as that vital reference point from which the mind wanders and is drawn back. Distraction cannot be seen as distraction unless there is some central focus to be distracted from. That is the frame of reference against which we can view the incessant changes and interruptions that go on all the time as a part of normal thinking.

Ancient Pali texts liken meditation to the process of taming a wild elephant. The procedure in those days was to tie a newly captured animal to a post with a good strong rope. When you do this, the elephant is not happy. He screams and tramples, and pulls against the rope for days. Finally it sinks through his skull that he can't get away, and he settles down. At this point you can begin to feed him and to handle him with some measure of safety. Eventually you can dispense with the rope and post altogether, and train your elephant for various tasks. Now you've got a tamed elephant that can be put to useful work. In this analogy the wild elephant is your wildly active mind, the rope is mindfulness, and the post is our object of meditation, our breathing. The tamed elephant who emerges from this process is a well-trained, concentrated mind that can then be used for the exceedingly tough job of piercing the layers of illusion that obscure reality. Meditation tames the mind.

The next question we need to address is: Why choose breathing as the primary object of meditation? Why not something a bit more interesting? Answers to this are numerous. A useful object of meditation should be one that promotes mindfulness. It should be portable, easily available, and cheap. It should also be something that will not embroil us in those states of mind from which we are trying to free ourselves, such as greed, anger, and delusion. Breathing satisfies all these criteria and more. Breathing is something common to every human being. We all carry it with us wherever we go. It is always there, constantly available, never ceasing from birth till death, and it costs nothing.

Breathing is a non-conceptual process, a thing that can be experienced directly without a need for thought. Furthermore, it is a very living process, an aspect of life that is in constant change. The breath moves in cycles—inhalation, exhalation, breathing in, and breathing out. Thus, it is a miniature model of life itself.

The sensation of breath is subtle, yet it is quite distinct when you learn to tune into it. It takes a bit of an effort to find it. Yet anybody can do it. You've got to work at it, but not too hard. For all these reasons, breathing makes an ideal object of meditation. Breathing is normally an involuntary process, proceeding at its own pace without a conscious will. Yet a single act of will can slow it down or speed it up. Make it long and smooth or short and choppy. The balance between involuntary breathing and forced manipulation of breath is quite delicate. And there are lessons to be learned here on the nature of will and desire. Then, too, that point at the tip of the nostril can be viewed as a sort of a window between the inner and outer worlds. It is a nexus point and energy-transfer spot where stuff from the outside world moves in and becomes a part of what we call "me," and where a part of "me" flows forth to merge with the outside world. There are lessons to be learned here about self-concept and how we form it.

Breath is a phenomenon common to all living things. A true experiential understanding of the process moves you closer to other living beings. It shows you your inherent connectedness with all of life. Finally, breathing is a present-time process. By that we mean it is always occurring in the here-and-now. We don't normally live in the present, of course. We spend most of our time caught up in memories of the past or looking ahead to the future, full of worries and plans. The breath has none of that "other-timeness." When we truly observe the breath, we are automatically placed in the present. We are pulled out of the morass of mental images and into a bare experience of the here-and-now. In this sense, breath is a living slice of reality. A mindful observation of such a miniature model of life itself leads to insights that are broadly applicable to the rest of our experience.

The first step in using the breath as an object of meditation is to find it. What you are looking for is the physical, tactile sensation of the air that passes in and out of the nostrils. This is usually just inside the tip of the nose. But the exact spot varies from one person to another, depending on the shape of the nose. To find your own point, take a quick deep breath and notice and point just inside the nose or on the upper lip where you have the most distinct sensation of passing air. Now exhale and notice the sensation at the same point. It is from this point that you will follow the whole passage of breath. Once you have located your own breath point with clarity, don't deviate from that spot. Use this single point in order to keep your attention fixed. Without having selected such a point, you will find yourself moving in and out of the nose, going up and down the windpipe, eternally chasing after the breath which you can never catch because it keeps changing, moving, and flowing.

If you ever sawed wood you already know the trick. As a carpenter, you don't stand there watching the saw blade going up and down. You would get dizzy. You fix your attention on the spot where the teeth of the blade dig into the wood. It is the only way you can saw a straight line. As a meditator, you focus your attention on that single spot of sensation inside the nose. From this vantage point, you watch the entire movement of breath with clear and collected attention. Make no attempt to control the breath. This is not a breathing exercise of the sort done in Yoga. Focus on the natural and spontaneous movement of the breath. Don't try to regulate it or emphasize it in any way. Most beginners have some trouble in this area. In order to help themselves focus on the sensation, they unconsciously accentuate their breathing. The result is a forced and unnatural effort that actually inhibits concentration rather than helping it. Don't increase the depth of your breath or its sound. This latter point is especially important in group meditation. Loud breathing can be a real annoyance to those around you. Just let the breath move naturally, as if you were asleep. Let go and allow the process to go along at its own rhythm.

This sounds easy, but it is trickier than you think. Do not be discouraged if you find your own will getting in the way. Just use that as an opportunity to observe the nature of conscious intention. Watch the delicate interrelation between the breath, the impulse to control the breath, and the impulse to cease controlling the breath. You may find it frustrating for a while, but it is highly profitable as a learning experience, and it is a passing phase. Eventually, the breathing process will move along under its own steam, and you will feel no impulse to manipulate it. At this point you will have learned a major lesson about your own compulsive need to control the universe.

Breathing, which seems so mundane and uninteresting at first glance, is actually an enormously complex and fascinating procedure. It is full of delicate variations, if you look. There is inhalation and exhalation, long breath and short breath, deep breath, shallow breath, smooth breath, and ragged breath. These categories combine with one another in subtle and intricate ways. Observe the breath closely. Really study it. You find enormous variations and a constant cycle of repeated patterns. It is like a symphony. Don't observe just the bare outline of the breath. There is more to see here than just an in-breath and an out-breath. Every breath has a beginning, middle and end. Every inhalation goes through a process of birth, growth, and death and every exhalation does the same. The depth and speed of your breathing changes according to your emotional state, the thought that flows through your mind, and the sounds you hear. Study these phenomena. You will find them fascinating.

This does not mean, however, that you should be sitting there having little conversations with yourself inside your head: "There is a short ragged breath and there is a deep long one. I wonder what's next?" No, that is not Vipassana. That is thinking. You will find this sort of thing happening, especially in the beginning. This too is a passing phase. Simply note the phenomenon and return your attention toward the observation of the sensation of breath. Mental distractions will happen again. But return your attention to your breath again, and again, and again, and again, for as long as it takes until it does not happen anymore.

When you first begin this procedure, expect to face some difficulties. Your mind will wander off constantly, darting around like a bumble bee and zooming off on wild tangents. Try not to worry. The monkey mind phenomenon is well known. It is something that every advanced meditator has had to deal with. They have pushed through it one way or another, and so can you. When it happens, just note the fact that you have been thinking, day-dreaming, worrying, or whatever. Gently, but firmly, without getting upset or judging yourself for straying, simply return to the simple physical sensation of the breath. Then do it again the next time, and again, and again, and again.

Somewhere in this process, you will come face to face with the sudden and shocking realization that you are completely crazy. Your mind is a shrieking, gibbering madhouse on wheels barreling pell-mell down the hill, utterly out of control and hopeless. No problem. You are not crazier than you were yesterday. It has always been this way, and you just never noticed. You are also no crazier than everybody else around you. The only real difference is that you have confronted the situation; they have not. So they still feel relatively comfortable. That does not mean that they are better off. Ignorance may be bliss, but it does not lead to Liberation. So don't let this realization unsettle you. It is a milestone actually, a sign of real progress. The very fact that you have looked at the problem straight in the eye means that you are on your way up and out of it.

In the wordless observation of the breath, there are two states to be avoided: thinking and sinking. The thinking mind manifests most clearly as the monkey mind phenomenon we have just being discussing. The sinking mind is almost the reverse. As a general term, sinking mind denotes any dimming of awareness. At its best, it is sort of a mental vacuum in which there is no thought, no observation of the breath, no awareness of anything. It is a gap, a formless mental gray area rather like a dreamless sleep. Sinking mind is a void. Avoid it.

Vipassana meditation is an active function. Concentration is a strong, energetic attention to one single item. Awareness is a bright clean alertness. *Samadhi* and *Sati*—these are the two faculties we wish to cultivate. And sinking mind contains neither. At its worst, it will put you to sleep. Even at its best it will simply waste your time.

When you find you have fallen into the state of sinking mind, just note the fact and return your attention to the sensation of breathing. Observe the tactile sensation of the in-breath. Feel the touch sensation of the out-breath. Breathe in, breathe out and watch what happens. When you have been doing that for some time—perhaps weeks or months—you will begin to sense the touch as a physical object. Simply continue the process; breathe in and breathe out. Watch what happens. As your concentration deepens you will have less and less trouble with monkey mind. Your breathing will slow down and you will track it more and more clearly, with fewer and fewer interruptions. You begin to experience a state of great calm in which you enjoy complete freedom from those things we called psychic irritants. No greed, lust, envy, jealousy, or hatred. Agitation goes away. Fear flees. These are beautiful, clear, blissful states of mind. They are temporary, and they will end when the meditation ends. Yet even these brief experiences will change your life. This is not Liberation, but these are stepping stones on the path that leads in that direction. Do not, however, expect instant bliss. Even these stepping stones take time and effort and patience.

The meditation experience is not a competition. There is a definite goal. But there is no timetable. What you are doing is digging your way deeper and deeper through layers of illusion toward realization of the supreme truth of existence. The process itself is fascinating and fulfilling. It can be enjoyed for its own sake. There is no need to rush.

At the end of a well-done meditation session you will feel a delightful freshness of mind. It is a peaceful, buoyant, and joyous energy which you can then apply to the problems of daily living. This in itself is reward enough. The purpose of meditation is not to deal with problems, however, and problem-solving ability is a fringe benefit and should be regarded as such. If you place too much emphasis on the problem-solving aspect, you will find your attention turning to those problems during the session sidetracking concentration. Don't think about your problems during your practice. Push them aside very gently.

Take a break from all that worrying and planning. Let your meditation be a complete vacation. Trust yourself, trust your own ability to deal with these issues later, using the energy and freshness of mind that you built up during your meditation. Trust yourself this way and it will actually occur.

Don't set goals for yourself that are too high to reach. Be gentle with yourself. You are trying to follow your own breathing continuously and without a break. That sounds easy enough, so you will have a tendency at the outset to push yourself to be scrupulous and exacting. This is unrealistic. Take time in small units instead. At the beginning of an inhalation, make the resolve to follow the breath just for the period of that one inhalation. Even this is not so easy, but at least it can be done. Then, at the start of the exhalation, resolve to follow the breath just for that one exhalation, all the way through. You will still fail repeatedly, but keep at it.

Every time you stumble, start over. Take it one breath at a time. This is the level of the game where you can actually win. Stick with it—fresh resolve with every breath cycle, tiny units of time. Observe each breath with care and precision, taking it one split second on top of another, with fresh resolve piled one on top of the other. In this way, continuous and unbroken awareness will eventually result.

Mindfulness of breathing is a present-time awareness. When you are doing it properly, you are aware only of what is occurring in the present. You don't look back, and you don't look forward. You forget about the last breath, and you don't anticipate the next one. When the inhalation is just beginning, you don't look ahead to the end of that inhalation. You don't skip forward to the exhalation which is to follow. You stay right there with what is actually taking place. The inhalation is beginning, and that's what you pay attention to; that and nothing else.

This meditation is a process of retraining the mind. The state you are aiming for is one in which you are totally aware of everything that is happening in your own perceptual universe, exactly the way it happens, exactly when it is happening; total, unbroken awareness in present time. This is an incredibly high goal, and not to be reached all at once. It takes practice, so we start small. We start by becoming totally aware of one small unit of time, just one single inhalation. And, when you succeed, you are on your way to a whole new experience of life.

# CHAPTER 8

# STRUCTURING YOUR MEDITATION

E verything up to this point has been theory. Now let's dive into the actual practice. Just how do we go about this thing called meditation?

First of all, you need to establish a formal practice schedule, a specific period when you will do Vipassana meditation and nothing else. When you were a baby, you did not know how to walk. Somebody went to a lot of trouble to teach you that skill. They dragged you by the arms. They gave you lots of encouragement, made you put one foot in front of the other until you could do it by yourself. Those periods of instruction constituted a formal practice in the art of walking.

In meditation, we follow the same basic procedure. We set aside a certain time, specifically devoted to developing this mental skill called mindfulness. We devote these times exclusively to that activity, and we structure our environment so there will be a minimum of distraction. This is not the easiest skill in the world to learn. We have spent our entire life developing mental habits that are really quite contrary to the ideal of uninterrupted mindfulness. Extricating ourselves from those habits requires a bit of strategy. As we said earlier, our minds are like cups of muddy water. The object of meditation is to clarify this sludge so that we can see what is going on in there. The best way to do that is just let it sit. Give it enough time and it will settle down. You wind up with clear water. In meditation, we set aside a specific time for this clarifying process. When viewed from the outside, it looks utterly useless. We sit there apparently as productive as a stone gargoyle. Inside, however, quite a bit is happening. The mental soup settles down, and we are left with a clarity of mind that prepares us to cope with the upcoming events of our lives.

That does not mean that we have to do anything to force this settling. It is a natural process that happens by itself. The very act of sitting still and being mindful causes this settling. In fact, any effort on our part to force this settling is counterproductive. That is repression, and it does not work. Try to force things out of the mind and you merely add energy to them. You may succeed temporarily, but in the long run you will only have made them stronger. They will hide in the unconscious until you are not watching, then they will leap out and leave you helpless to fight them off.

The best way to clarify the mental fluid is to just let it settle all by itself. Don't add any energy to the situation. Just mindfully watch the mud swirl, without any involvement in the process. Then, when it settles at last, it will stay settled. We exert energy in meditation, but not force. Our only effort is gentle, patient mindfulness.

The meditation period is like a cross-section of your whole day. Everything that happens to you is stored away in the mind in some form, mental or emotional. During normal activity, you get so caught up in the press of events that the basic issues with which you are dealing are seldom thoroughly handled. They become buried in the unconscious, where they seethe and foam and fester. Then you wonder where all that tension came from. All of this material comes forth in one form or another during your meditation. You get a chance to look at it, see it for what it is, and let it go.

We set up a formal meditation period in order to create a conducive environment for this release. We reestablish our mindfulness at regular intervals. We withdraw from those events which constantly stimulate the mind. We back out of all that activity that prods the emotions. We go off to a quiet place and we sit still, and it all comes bubbling out. Then it goes away. The net effect is like recharging a battery. Meditation recharges your mindfulness.

## WHERE TO SIT?

Find yourself a quiet place, a secluded place, a place where you will be alone. It doesn't have to be some ideal spot in the middle of a forest. That's nearly impossible for most of us, but it should be a place where you feel comfortable, and where you won't be disturbed. It should also be a place where you won't feel on display. You want all of your attention free for meditation, not wasted on worries about how you look to others. Try to pick a spot that is as quiet as possible. It doesn't have to be a soundproof room, but there are certain noises that are highly distracting, and they should be avoided. Music and talking are about the worst. The mind tends to be sucked in by these sounds in an uncontrollable manner, and there goes your concentration.

There are certain traditional aids that you can employ to set the proper mood. A darkened room with a candle is nice. Incense is nice. A little bell to start and end your sessions is nice. These are paraphernalia, though. They provide encouragement to some people, but they are by no means essential to the practice.

You will probably find it helpful to sit in the same place each time. A special spot reserved for meditation and nothing else is an aid for most people. You soon come to associate that spot with the tranquility of deep concentration, and that association helps you to reach deep states more quickly. The main thing is to sit in a place that you feel is conducive to your own practice. That requires a bit of experimentation. Try several spots until you find one where you feel comfortable. You only need to find a place where you don't feel self-conscious, and where you can meditate without undue distraction.

Many people find it helpful and supportive to sit with a group of other meditators. The discipline of regular practice is essential, and most people find it easier to sit regularly if they are bolstered by a commitment to a group sitting schedule. You've given your word, and you know you are expected to keep it. Thus, the "I'm too busy" syndrome is cleverly skirted. You may be able to locate a group of practicing meditators in your own area. It doesn't matter if they practice a different form of meditation, so long as it's one of the silent forms. On the other hand, you also should try to be self-sufficient in your practice. Don't rely on the presence of a group as your sole motivation to sit. Properly done, sitting is a pleasure. Use the group as an aid, not as a crutch.

WHEN TO SIT?

The most important rule here is this: When it comes to sitting, the description of Buddhism as the Middle Way applies. Don't overdo it. Don't underdo it. This doesn't mean you just sit whenever the whim strikes you. It means you set up a practice schedule and keep to it with a gentle, patient tenacity. Setting up a schedule acts as an encouragement. If, however, you find that your schedule has ceased to be an encouragement and become a burden, then something is wrong. Meditation is not a duty, nor an obligation.

Meditation is a psychological activity. You will be dealing with the raw stuff of feelings and emotions. Consequently, it is an activity which is very sensitive to the attitude with which you approach each session. What you expect is what you are most likely to get. Your practice will therefore go best when you are looking forward to sitting. If you sit down expecting grinding drudgery, that is probably what will occur. So set up a daily pattern that you can live with. Make it reasonable. Make it fit with the rest of your life. And if it starts to feel like you're on an uphill treadmill toward liberation, then change something.

First thing in the morning is a great time to meditate. Your mind is fresh then, before you've gotten yourself buried in responsibilities. Morning meditation is a fine way to start your day. It tunes you up and gets you ready to deal with things efficiently. You cruise through the rest of the day just a bit more lightly. Be sure you are thoroughly awake, though. You won't make much progress if you are sitting there nodding off, so get enough sleep. Wash your face, or shower before you begin. You may want to do a bit of exercise beforehand to get the circulation flowing. Do whatever you need to do in order to wake up fully, then sit down to meditate. Do not, however, let yourself get hung up in the day's activities. It's just too easy to forget to sit. Make meditation the first major thing you do in the morning.

The evening is another good time for practice. Your mind is full of all the mental rubbish that you have accumulated during the day, and it is great to get rid of that burden before you sleep. Your meditation will cleanse and rejuvenate your mind. Reestablish your mindfulness and your sleep will be real sleep.

When you first start meditation, once a day is enough. If

you feel like meditating more, that's fine, but don't overdo it. There's a burn-out phenomenon we often see in new meditators. They dive right into the practice fifteen hours a day for a couple of weeks, and then the real world catches up with them. They decide that this meditation business just takes too much time. Too many sacrifices are required. They haven't got time for all of this. Don't fall into that trap. Don't burn yourself out the first week. Make haste slowly. Make your effort consistent and steady. Give yourself time to incorporate the meditation practice into your life, and let your practice grow gradually and gently.

As your interest in meditation grows, you'll find yourself making more room in your schedule for practice. It's a spontaneous phenomenon, and it happens pretty much by itself—no force necessary.

Seasoned meditators manage three or four hours of practice a day. They live ordinary lives in the day-to-day world, and they still squeeze it all in. And they enjoy it. It comes naturally.

## How Long To Sit?

A similar rule applies here: sit as long as you can, but don't overdo it. Most beginners start with twenty or thirty minutes. Initially, it's difficult to sit longer than that with profit. The posture is unfamiliar to Westerners, and it takes a bit of time for the body to adjust. The mental skills are equally unfamiliar, and that adjustment takes time, too.

As you grow accustomed to the procedure, you can extend your meditation little by little. We recommend that after a year or so of steady practice you should be sitting comfortably for an hour at a time.

Here is an important point, though: Vipassana meditation

is not a form of asceticism. Self-mortification is not the goal. We are trying to cultivate mindfulness, not pain. Some pain is inevitable, especially in the legs. We will thoroughly cover pain, and how to handle it, in Chapter 10. There are special techniques and attitudes which you will learn for dealing with discomfort. The point to be made here is this: This is not a grim endurance contest. You don't need to prove anything to anybody. So don't force yourself to sit with excruciating pain just to be able to say that you sat for an hour. That is a useless exercise in ego. And don't overdo it in the beginning. Know your limitations, and don't condemn yourself for not being able to sit forever, like a rock.

As meditation becomes more and more a part of your life, you can extend your sessions beyond an hour. As a general rule, just determine what is a comfortable length of time for you at this point in your life. Then sit five minutes longer than that.

There is no hard and fast rule about length of time for sitting. Even if you have established a firm minimum, there may be days when it is physically impossible for you to sit that long. That doesn't mean that you should just cancel the whole idea for that day. It's crucial to sit regularly. Even ten minutes of meditation can be very beneficial.

Incidentally, you decide on the length of your session before you meditate. Don't do it while you are meditating. It's too easy to give in to restlessness that way, and restlessness is one of the main items that we want to learn to mindfully observe. So choose a realistic length of time, and then stick to it.

You can use a watch to time your session, but don't peek at it every two minutes to see how you are doing. Your concentration will be completely lost, and agitation will set in.

You'll find yourself hoping to get up before the session is over. That's not meditation—that's clock watching. Don't look at the clock until you think the whole meditation period has passed. Actually, you don't need to consult the clock at all, at least not every time you meditate. In general, you should be sitting for as long as you want to sit. There is no magic length of time. It is best, however, to set yourself a minimum length of time. If you haven't predetermined a minimum, you'll find yourself prone to short sessions. You'll bolt every time something unpleasant comes up or whenever you feel restless. That's no good. These experiences are some of the most profitable a meditator can face, but only if you sit through them. You've got to learn to observe them calmly and clearly. Look at them mindfully. When you've done that enough times, they lose their hold on you. You see them for what they are: just impulses, arising and passing away, just part of the passing show. Your life smoothes out beautifully as a consequence.

"Discipline" is a difficult word for most of us. It conjures up images of somebody standing over you with a stick, telling you that you're wrong. But self-discipline is different. It's the skill of seeing through the hollow shouting of your own impulses and piercing their secret. They have no power over you. It's all a show, a deception. Your urges scream and bluster at you; they cajole; they coax; they threaten; but they really carry no stick at all. You give in out of habit. You give in because you never really bother to look beyond the threat. It is all empty back there. There is only one way to learn this lesson, though. The words on this page won't do it. But look within and watch the stuff coming up—restlessness, anxiety, impatience, pain—just watch it come up and don't get involved. Much to your surprise, it will simply go away. It rises, it passes away. As simple as that. There is another word for self-discipline. It is patience.

# CHAPTER 9

# SET UP EXERCISES

In Theravada Buddhist countries, it is traditional to begin each meditation session with the recitation of a certain set of formulas. An American audience is likely to take one glance at these invocations and to dismiss them as harmless rituals and nothing more. These so-called rituals, however, have been devised and refined by a set of pragmatic and dedicated men and women, and they have a thoroughly practical purpose. They are therefore worthy of deeper inspection.

The Buddha was considered contrary in his own day. He was born into an intensely over-ritualized society, and his ideas appeared thoroughly iconoclastic to the established hierarchy of his own era. On numerous occasions, he disavowed the use of rituals for their own sake, and he was quite adamant about it. This does not mean that ritual has no use. It means that ritual by itself, performed strictly for its own sake, will not get you out of the trap. Indeed, such performance is a part of the trap. If you believe that mere recitation of words will save you, then you only increase your own dependence on words and concepts. This moves you away from the wordless perception of reality rather than toward it. Therefore, the formulae which follow must be practiced with a clear understanding of what they are and why they work. They are not prayers, and they are not mantras. They are not magical incantations. They are psychological cleansing devices which require active mental

97

participation in order to be effective. Mumbled words without intention are useless. Vipassana meditation is a delicate psychological activity, and the mental set of the practitioner is crucial to its success. The technique works best in an atmosphere of calm, benevolent confidence. And these recitations have been designed to foster those attitudes. Correctly used, they can act as a helpful tool on the path to liberation.

## THE THREEFOLD GUIDANCE

Meditation is a tough job. It is an inherently solitary activity. One person battles against enormously powerful forces, part of the very structure of the mind doing the meditating. When you really get into it, you will eventually find yourself confronted with a shocking realization. One day you will look inside and realize the full enormity of what you are actually up against. What you are struggling to pierce looks like a solid wall so tightly knit that not a single ray of light shines through. You find yourself sitting there, staring at this edifice and you say to yourself, "That? I am supposed to get past that? But it's impossible! That is all there is. That is the whole world. That is what everything means, and that is what I use to define myself and to understand everything around me, and if I take that away the whole world will fall apart and I will die. I cannot get through that. I just can't."

It is a very scary feeling, a very lonely feeling. You feel like, "Here I am, all alone, trying to punch away something so huge it is beyond conception." To counteract this feeling, it is useful to know that you are not alone. Others have passed this way before. They have confronted that same barrier, and they have pushed their way through to the light. They have laid out the rules by which the job can be done, and they have banded together into a brotherhood for mutual encouragement and support. The Buddha found his way through this very same wall, and after him came many others. He left clear instructions in the form of the Dhamma to guide us along the same path. And he founded the Sangha, the brotherhood of monks to preserve that path and to keep each other on it. You are not alone, and the situation is not hopeless.

Meditation takes energy. You need courage to confront some pretty difficult mental phenomena and the determination to sit through various unpleasant mental states. Laziness just will not serve. In order to pump up your energy for the job, repeat the following statements to yourself. Feel the intention you put into them. Mean what you say.

"I am about to tread the very same path that has been walked by the Buddha and by his great and holy disciples. An indolent person cannot follow that path. May my energy prevail. May I succeed."

## Universal Loving Kindness

Vipassana meditation is an exercise in mindfulness, that is, in egoless awareness. It is a procedure in which the ego will be eradicated by the penetrating gaze of mindfulness. The practitioner begins this process with the ego in full command of mind and body. Then, as mindfulness watches the ego function, it penetrates to the roots of the mechanics of ego and extinguishes ego piece by piece. There is a full blown Catch-22 in all this, however. Mindfulness is egoless awareness. If we start with ego in full control, how do we put enough mindfulness there at the beginning to get the job started? There is always some mindfulness present in any moment. The real problem is to gather enough of it to be effective. To do this we can use a clever tactic. We can weaken those aspects of ego which do the most harm, so that mindfulness will have less resistance to overcome.

Greed and hatred are the prime manifestations of the ego process. To the extent that grasping and rejecting are present in the mind, mindfulness will have a very rough time. The results of this are easy to see. If you sit down to meditate while you are in the grip of some strong obsessive attachment, you will find that you will get nowhere. If you are all hung up in your latest scheme to make more money, you probably will spend most of your meditation period doing nothing but thinking about it. If you are in a black fury over some recent insult, that will occupy your mind just as fully. There is only so much time in one day, and your meditation minutes are precious. It is best not to waste them. The Theravada tradition has developed a useful tool which will allow you to remove these barriers from your mind at least temporarily, so that you can get on with the job of removing their roots permanently.

You can use one idea to cancel another. You can balance a negative emotion by instilling a positive one. Giving is the opposite of greed. Benevolence is the opposite of hatred. Understand clearly now: this is not an attempt to liberate yourself by autohypnosis. You cannot condition Enlightenment. Nibbana is an unconditioned state. A liberated person will indeed be generous and benevolent, but not because he has been conditioned to be so. He will be so purely as a manifestation of his own basic nature, which is no longer inhibited by ego. So this is not conditioning. This is rather psychological medicine. If you take this medicine according to directions, it will bring temporary relief from the symptoms of the malady from which you are currently suffering. Then you can get to work in earnest on the illness itself.

You start out by banishing thoughts of self-hatred and self-condemnation. You allow good feelings and good wishes first to flow to yourself, which is relatively easy. Then you do the same for those people closest to you. Gradually, you work outward from your own circle of intimates until you can direct a flow of those same emotions to your enemies and to all living beings everywhere. Correctly done, this can be a powerful and transformative exercise in itself.

At the beginning of each meditation session, say the following sentences to yourself. Really feel the intention:

*May I be well, happy, and peaceful. May no harm come to me. May no difficulties come to me. May no problems come to me. May I always meet with success. May I also have patience, courage, understanding, and determination to meet and overcome inevitable difficulties, problems, and failures in life.*

*May my parents be well, happy, and peaceful. May no harm come to them. May no difficulties come to them. May no problems come to them. May they always meet with success. May they also have patience, courage, understanding, and determination to meet and overcome inevitable difficulties, problems, and failures in life.*

*May my teachers be well, happy, and peaceful. May no harm come to them. May no difficulties come to them. May no problems come to them. May they always meet with success. May they also have patience, courage, understanding, and determination to meet and overcome inevitable difficulties, problems, and failures in life.*

101

*May my relatives be well, happy, and peaceful. May no harm come to them. May no difficulties come to them. May no problems come to them. May they always meet with success. May they also have patience, courage, understanding, and determination to meet and overcome inevitable difficulties, problems, and failures in life.*

*May my friends be well, happy, and peaceful. May no harm come to them. May no difficulties come to them. May no problems come to them. May they always meet with success. May they also have patience, courage, understanding, and determination to meet and overcome inevitable difficulties, problems, and failures in life.*

*May all persons who are strangers to me be well, happy, and peaceful. May no harm come to them. May no difficulties come to them. May no problems come to them. May they always meet with success. May they also have patience, courage, understanding, and determination to meet and overcome inevitable difficulties, problems, and failures in life.*

*May my enemies be well, happy, and peaceful. May no harm come to them. May no difficulties come to them. May no problems come to them. May they always meet with success. May they also have patience, courage, understanding, and determination to meet and overcome inevitable difficulties, problems, and failures in life.*

*May all living beings be well, happy, and peaceful. May no harm come to them. May no difficulties come to them. May no problems come to them. May they always meet with success. May they also have patience, courage, understanding, and determination to meet and overcome inevitable difficulties, problems, and failures in life.*

Once you have completed these recitations, lay aside all your troubles and conflicts for the period of practice. Just drop the whole bundle. If they come back into your meditation later, just treat them as what they are, distractions.

The practice of Universal Loving Kindness is also recommended for bedtime and just after arising. It is said to help you sleep well and to prevent nightmares. It also makes it easier to get up in the morning. And it makes you more friendly and open toward everybody, friend or foe, human or otherwise.

The most damaging psychic irritant arising in the mind, particularly at the time when the mind is quiet, is resentment. You may experience indignation remembering some incident that caused you psychological and physical pain. This experience can cause you uneasiness, tension, agitation, and worry. You might not be able to go on sitting and experiencing this state of mind. Therefore, we strongly recommend that you should start your meditation with generating Universal Loving Kindness.

You may wonder how we can wish: "May my *enemies* be well, happy and peaceful. May no harm come to them; may no difficulties come to them; may no problem come to them; may they always meet with success. May they also have patience, courage, understanding and determination to meet and overcome inevitable difficulties, problems, and failures in life."

You must remember that you practice loving kindness for the purification of your own mind, just as you practice meditation for your own attainment of peace and liberation from pain and suffering. As you practice loving kindness within yourself, you can behave in a most friendly manner without biases, prejudices, discrimination, or hate. Your

103

noble behavior enables you to help others in a most practical manner to reduce their pain and suffering. It is compassionate people who can help others. Compassion is a manifestation of loving kindness in action, for one who does not have loving kindness cannot help others. Noble behavior means behaving in a most friendly manner. Behavior includes your thought, speech, and actions. If this triple mode of expression of your behavior is contradictory, then something is wrong, and contradictory behavior cannot be noble behavior. On the other hand, pragmatically speaking, it is much better to cultivate the noble thought, "May all beings be happy minded" than the thought, "I hate him." Our noble thought will one day express itself in noble behavior and our spiteful thought in evil behavior.

Remember that your thoughts are transformed into speech and action in order to bring the expected result. Thought translated into action is capable of producing a tangible result. You should always speak and do things with mindfulness of loving kindness. While speaking of loving kindness, if you act or speak in a diametrically opposite way you will be reproached by the wise. As mindfulness of loving kindness develops, your thoughts, words, and deeds should be gentle, pleasant, meaningful, truthful, and beneficial to you as well as to others. If your thoughts, words, or deeds cause harm to you, to others, or to both, then you must ask yourself whether you are really mindful of loving kindness.

For all practical purposes, if all of your enemies are well, happy and peaceful, they would not be your enemies. If they are free from problems, pain, suffering, affliction, neurosis, psychosis, paranoia, fear, tension, anxiety, etc., they would not be your enemies. Your practical solution toward your enemies is to help them to overcome their problems, so you can live in peace and happiness. In fact, if you can, you should fill the minds of all your enemies with loving kindness and make all of them realize the true meaning of peace, so you can live in peace and happiness. The more they are in neurosis, psychosis, fear, tension, anxiety, etc., the more trouble, pain, and suffering they can bring to the world. If you could convert a vicious and wicked person into a holy and saintly individual, you would perform a miracle. Let us cultivate adequate wisdom and loving kindness within ourselves to convert evil minds to saintly minds.

When you hate somebody, you think, "Let him be ugly. Let him lie in pain. Let him have no prosperity. Let him not be rich. Let him not be famous. Let him have no friends. Let him, after death, reappear in an unhappy state of deprivation in a bad destination in perdition." However, what actually happens is that your own body generates such harmful chemistry that you experience pain, increased heart beat, tension, change of facial expression, loss of appetite, deprivation of sleep and appear very unpleasant to others. You go through the same things you wish for your enemy. Also you cannot see the truth as it is. Your mind is like boiling water. Or you are like a patient suffering from jaundice to whom any delicious food tastes bland. Similarly, you cannot appreciate somebody's appearance, achievement, success, etc. As long as this condition exists, you cannot meditate well.

Therefore, we recommend very strongly that you practice loving kindness before you start your serious practice of meditation. Repeat the preceding passages very mindfully and meaningfully. As you recite these passages, feel true loving kindness within yourself first and then share it with others, for you cannot share with others what you do not have within yourself.

Remember, though, these are not magic formulas. They don't work by themselves. If you use them as such, you will simply waste time and energy. But if you truly participate in these statements and invest them with your own energy, they will serve you well. Give them a try. See for yourself.

# CHAPTER 10

## DEALING WITH PROBLEMS

You are going to run into problems in your meditation. Everybody does. Problems come in all shapes and sizes, and the only thing you can be absolutely certain about is that you will have some. The main trick in dealing with obstacles is to adopt the right attitude. Difficulties are an integral part of your practice. They aren't something to be avoided. They are something to be used. They provide invaluable opportunities for learning.

The reason we are all stuck in life's mud is that we ceaselessly run from our problems and after our desires. Meditation provides us with a laboratory situation in which we can examine this syndrome and devise strategies for dealing with it. The various snags and hassles that arise during meditation are grist for the mill. They are the material with which we work. There is no pleasure without some degree of pain. There is no pain without some amount of pleasure. Life is composed of joys and miseries. They go hand in hand. Meditation is no exception. You will experience good times and bad times, ecstasies and frightening times.

So don't be surprised when you hit some experience that feels like a brick wall. Don't think you are special. Every seasoned meditator has had his own brick walls. They come up again and again. Just expect them and be ready to cope. Your ability to cope with trouble depends upon your attitude. If you can learn to regard these hassles as opportunities, as chances to develop in your practice, you'll make progress. Your ability to deal with some issue that arises in meditation will carry over into the rest of your life and allow you to smooth out the big issues that really bother you. If you try to avoid each piece of nastiness that arises in meditation, you are simply reinforcing the habit that has already made life seem so unbearable at times.

It is essential to learn to confront the less pleasant aspects of existence. Our job as meditators is to learn to be patient with ourselves, to see ourselves in an unbiased way, complete with all our sorrows and inadequacies. We have to learn to be kind to ourselves. In the long run, avoiding unpleasantness is a very unkind thing to do to yourself. Paradoxically, kindness entails confronting unpleasantness when it arises. One popular human strategy for dealing with difficulty is autosuggestion: when something nasty pops up, you convince yourself it is not there, or you convince yourself it is pleasant rather than unpleasant. The Buddha's tactic is quite the reverse. Rather than hide it or disguise it, the Buddha's teaching urges you to examine it to death. Buddhism advises you not to implant feelings that you don't really have or avoid feelings that you do have. If you are miserable you are miserable; that is the reality, that is what is happening, so confront that. Look it square in the eye without flinching. When you are having a bad time, examine that badness, observe it mindfully, study the phenomenon and learn its mechanics. The way out of a trap is to study the trap itself, learn how it is built. You do this by taking the thing apart piece by piece. The trap can't trap you if it has been taken to pieces. The result is freedom.

This point is essential, but it is one of the least understood aspects of Buddhist philosophy. Those who have studied

Buddhism superficially are quick to conclude that it is a pessimistic set of teachings, always harping on unpleasant things like suffering, always urging us to confront the uncomfortable realities of pain, death, and illness. Buddhist thinkers do not regard themselves as pessimists—quite the opposite, actually. Pain exists in the universe; some measure of it is unavoidable. Learning to deal with it is not pessimism, but a very pragmatic form of optimism. How would you deal with the death of your spouse? How would you feel if you lost your mother tomorrow? Or your sister or your closest friend? Suppose you lost your job, your savings, and the use of your legs, on the same day; could you face the prospect of spending the rest of your life in a wheelchair? How are you going to cope with the pain of terminal cancer if you contract it, and how will you deal with your own death, when that approaches? You may escape most of these misfortunes, but you won't escape all of them. Most of us lose friends and relatives at some time during our lives; all of us get sick now and then; and all of us will die someday. You can suffer through things like that or you can face them openly—the choice is yours.

Pain is inevitable, suffering is not. Pain and suffering are two different animals. If any of these tragedies strike you in your present state of mind, you will suffer. The habit patterns that presently control your mind will lock you into that suffering and there will be no escape. A bit of time spent in learning alternatives to those habit patterns is time well invested. Most human beings spend all their energies devising ways to increase their pleasure and decrease their pain. Buddhism does not advise that you cease this activity altogether. Money and security are fine. Pain should be avoided whenever possible. Nobody is telling you to give away all your possessions or seek out needless pain, but Buddhism does advise you to invest some of your time and energy in learning to deal with unpleasantness, because some pain is unavoidable. When you see a truck bearing down on you, by all means jump out of the way. But spend some time in meditation, too. Learning to deal with discomfort is the only way you'll be ready to handle the truck you didn't see.

Problems will arise in your practice. Some of them will be physical, some will be emotional, and some will be attitudinal. All of them can be confronted and each has its own specific response. All of them are opportunities to free yourself.

PROBLEM 1—*Physical Pain*

Nobody likes pain, yet everybody has some at one time or another. It is one of life's most common experiences and is bound to arise in your meditation in one form or another.

Handling pain is a two-stage process. First, get rid of the pain, if possible, or at least get rid of it as much as possible. Then, if some pain lingers, use it as an object of meditation. The first step is physical handling. Maybe the pain is an illness of one sort or another, a headache, fever, bruises, or whatever. In this case, employ standard medical treatments before you sit down to meditate: take your medicine, apply your liniment, do whatever you ordinarily would do. Then there are certain pains that are specific to the seated posture. If you never spend much time sitting cross-legged on the floor, there will be an adjustment period. Some discomfort is nearly inevitable. According to where the pain is, there are specific remedies. If the pain is in the leg or knees, check your pants. If they are tight or made of thick material, that could be the problem. Try to change it. Check your cushion, too. It should be about three inches in height when compressed. If the pain is around your waist, try loosening your belt. Loosen the waistband of your pants if that is necessary. If you experience pain in your lower back, your posture is probably at fault. Slouching will never be comfortable, so straighten up. Don't be tight or rigid, but do keep your spine erect. Pain in the neck or upper back has several sources. The first is improper hand position. Your hands should be resting comfortably in your lap. Don't pull them up to your waist. Relax your arms and your neck muscles. Don't let your head droop forward. Keep it up and aligned with the rest of the spine.

After you have made all these various adjustments, you may find you still have some lingering pain. If that is the case, try step two. Make the pain your object of meditation. Don't jump up and don't get excited. Just observe the pain mindfully. When the pain becomes demanding, you will find it pulling your attention off the breath. Don't fight back. Just let your attention slide easily over onto the simple sensation. Go into the pain fully. Don't block the experience. Explore the feeling. Get beyond your avoiding reaction and go into the pure sensations that lie below that. You will discover that there are two things present. The first is the simple sensation—pain itself. Second is your resistance to that sensation. Resistance reaction is partly mental and partly physical. The physical part consists of tensing the muscles in and around the painful area. Relax those muscles. Take them one by one and relax each one very thoroughly. This step alone will probably diminish the pain significantly. Then go after the mental side of the resistance. Just as you are tensing physically, you are also tensing psychologically. You are clamping down mentally on the sensation of pain, trying to screen it off and reject it from consciousness. The rejection is a wordless, "I don't like this feeling" or "go away" attitude. It is very subtle. But it is there, and you can find it if you really look. Locate it and relax that, too.

That last part is more subtle. There are really no human words to describe this action precisely. The best way to get a handle on it is by analogy. Examine what you did to those tight muscles and transfer that same action over to the mental sphere; relax the mind in the same way that you relax the body. Buddhism recognizes that body and mind are tightly linked. This is so true that many people will not see this as a two-step procedure. For them to relax the body is to relax the mind and vice versa. These people will experience the entire relaxation, mental and physical, as a single process. In any case, just let go completely till your awareness slows down past that barrier of resistance and relaxes into the pure flowing sensation beneath. The resistance was a barrier which you yourself erected. It was a gap, a sense of distance between self and others. It was a borderline between "me" and "the pain." Dissolve that barrier, and separation vanishes. You slow down into that sea of surging sensation and you merge with the pain. You become the pain. You watch its ebb and flow and something surprising happens. It no longer hurts. Suffering is gone. Only the pain remains, an experience, nothing more. The "me" who was being hurt has gone. The result is freedom from pain.

This is an incremental process. In the beginning, you can expect to succeed with small pains and be defeated by big ones. Like most of our skills, it grows with practice. The more you practice, the more pain you can handle. Please understand fully. There is no masochism being advocated here. Self-mortification is not the point. This is an exercise in awareness, not in self-torture. If the pain becomes excruciating, go ahead and move, but move slowly and mindfully.

112

Observe your movements. See how it feels to move. Watch what it does to the pain. Watch the pain diminish. Try not to move too much, though. The less you move, the easier it is to remain fully mindful. New meditators sometimes say they have trouble remaining mindful when pain is present. This difficulty stems from a misunderstanding. These students are conceiving mindfulness as something distinct from the experience of pain. It is not. Mindfulness never exists by itself. It always has some object and one object is as good as another. Pain is a mental state. You can be mindful of pain just as you are mindful of breathing.

The rules we covered in Chapter 4 apply to pain just as they apply to any other mental state. You must be careful not to reach beyond the sensation and not to fall short of it. Don't add anything to it, and don't miss any part of it. Don't muddy the pure experience with concepts or pictures or discursive thinking. And keep your awareness right in the present time, right with the pain, so that you won't miss its beginning or its end. Pain not viewed in the clear light of mindfulness gives rise to emotional reactions like fear, anxiety, or anger. If it is properly viewed, we have no such reaction. It will be just sensation, just simple energy. Once you have learned this technique with physical pain, you can then generalize it in the rest of your life. You can use it on any unpleasant sensation. What works on pain will work on anxiety or chronic depression as well. This technique is one of life's most useful and applicable skills. It is patience.

PROBLEM 2—*Legs Going to Sleep*

It is very common for beginners to have their legs fall asleep or go numb during meditation. They are simply not accustomed to the cross-legged posture. Some people get very anxious about this. They feel they must get up and move around. A few are completely convinced that they will get gangrene from lack of circulation. Numbness in the leg is nothing to worry about. It is caused by nerve-pinch, not by lack of circulation. You can't damage the tissues of your legs by sitting. So relax. When your legs fall asleep in meditation, just mindfully observe the phenomenon. Examine what it feels like. It may be sort of uncomfortable, but it is not painful unless you tense up. Just stay calm and watch it. It does not matter if your legs go numb and stay that way for the whole period. After you have meditated for some time, that numbness will gradually disappear. Your body simply adjusts to daily practice. Then you can sit for very long sessions with no numbness whatever.

## PROBLEM 3—*Odd Sensations*

People experience all manner of varied phenomena in meditation. Some people get itches. Others feel tingling, deep relaxation, a feeling of lightness or a floating sensation. You may feel yourself growing or shrinking or rising up in the air. Beginners often get quite excited over such sensations. Don't worry, you are not likely to levitate any time soon. As relaxation sets in, the nervous system simply begins to pass sensory signals more efficiently. Large amounts of previously blocked sensory data can pour through, giving rise to all kinds of unique sensations. It does not signify anything in particular. It is just sensation. So simply employ the normal technique. Watch it come up and watch it pass away. Don't get involved.

## PROBLEM 4—*Drowsiness*

It is quite common to experience drowsiness during meditation. You become very calm and relaxed. That is exactly what is supposed to happen. Unfortunately, we ordinarily experience this lovely state only when we are falling asleep, and we associate it with that process. So naturally, you begin to drift off. When you find this happening, apply your mindfulness to the state of drowsiness itself. Drowsiness has certain definite characteristics. It does certain things to your thought process. Find out what. It has certain bodily feelings associated with it. Locate those.

This inquisitive awareness is the direct opposite of drowsiness, and will evaporate it. If it does not, then you should suspect a physical cause of your sleepiness. Search that out and handle it. If you have just eaten a large meal, that could be the cause. It is best to eat lightly if you are about to meditate. Or wait an hour after a big meal. And don't overlook the obvious either. If you have been out loading bricks all day, you are naturally going to be tired. The same is true if you only got a few hours of sleep the night before. Take care of your body's physical needs. Then meditate. Do not give in to sleepiness. Stay awake and mindful, for sleep and meditative concentration are two diametrically opposed experiences. You will not gain any new insight from sleep, but only from meditation. If you are very sleepy then take a deep breath and hold it as long as you can. Then breathe out slowly. Take another deep breath again, hold it as long as you can and breathe out slowly. Repeat this exercise until your body warms up and sleepiness fades away. Then return to your breath.

PROBLEM 5—*Inability to Concentrate*

An overactive, jumping attention is something that everybody experiences from time to time. It is generally handled by the techniques presented in the chapter on distractions. You should also be informed, however, that there are certain external factors which contribute to this phenomenon. And these are best handled by simple adjustments in your schedule. Mental images are powerful entities. They can remain in the mind for long periods. All of the storytelling arts are direct manipulation of such material, and if the writer has done his job well, the characters and images presented will have a powerful and lingering effect on the mind. If you have been to the best movie of the year, the meditation which follows is going to be full of those images. If you are halfway through the scariest horror novel you ever read, your meditation is going to be full of monsters. So switch the order of events. Do your meditation first. Then read or go to the movies.

Another influential factor is your own emotional state. If there is some real conflict in your life, that agitation will carry over into meditation. Try to resolve your immediate daily conflicts before meditation when you can. Your life will run more smoothly, and you won't be pondering uselessly in your practice. But don't use this advice as a way to avoid meditation. Sometimes you can't resolve every issue before you sit. Just go ahead and sit anyway. Use your meditation to let go of all the egocentric attitudes that keep you trapped within your own limited viewpoint. Your problems will resolve much more easily thereafter. And then there are those days when it seems that the mind will never rest, but you can't locate any apparent cause. Remember the cyclic alternation we spoke of earlier. Meditation goes in cycles. You have good days and you have bad days.

Vipassana meditation is primarily an exercise in awareness. Emptying the mind is not as important as being mindful of what the mind is doing. If you are frantic and you can't do a thing to stop it, just observe. It is all you. The result will be one more step forward in your journey of self-exploration. Above all, don't get frustrated over the nonstop chatter of your mind. That babble is just one more thing to be mindful of.

## PROBLEM 6—*Boredom*

It is difficult to imagine anything more inherently boring than sitting still for an hour with nothing to do but feel the air going in and out of your nose. You are going to run into boredom repeatedly in your meditation. Everybody does. Boredom is a mental state and should be treated as such. A few simple strategies will help you to cope.

### *Tactic A: Reestablish true mindfulness.*

If the breath seems an exceedingly dull thing to observe over and over, you may rest assured of one thing: you have ceased to observe the process with true mindfulness. Mindfulness is never boring. Look again. Don't assume that you know what breath is. Don't take it for granted that you have already seen everything there is to see. If you do, you are conceptualizing the process. You are not observing its living reality. When you are clearly mindful of the breath or of anything else, it is never boring. Mindfulness looks at everything with the eyes of a child, with a sense of wonder. Mindfulness sees every moment as if it were the first and the only moment in the universe. So look again.

### *Tactic B: Observe your mental state.*

Look at your state of boredom mindfully. What is boredom? Where is boredom? What does it feel like? What are its mental components? Does it have any physical feeling? What does it do to your thought process? Take a fresh look at boredom, as if you have never experienced that state before.

## PROBLEM 7—*Fear*

States of fear sometimes arise during meditation for no discernible reason. It is a common phenomenon, and there can be a number of causes. You may be experiencing the effect of something repressed long ago. Remember, thoughts arise first in the unconscious. The emotional contents of a thought complex often leak through into your conscious awareness long before the thought itself surfaces. If you sit through the fear, the memory itself may bubble up to a point where you can endure it. Or you may be dealing directly with that fear which we all fear: "fear of the unknown." At some point in your meditation career you will be struck with the seriousness of what you are actually doing. You are tearing down the wall of illusion you have always used to explain life to yourself and to shield yourself from the intense flame of reality. You are about to meet ultimate truth face to face. That is scary. But it has to be dealt with eventually. Go ahead and dive right in.

A third possibility: the fear that you are feeling may be self-generated. It may be arising out of unskillful concentration. You may have set an unconscious program to "examine what comes up." Thus, when a frightening fantasy arises, concentration locks onto it and the fantasy feeds on the energy of your attention and grows. The real problem here is that mindfulness is weak. If mindfulness was strongly developed, it would notice this switch of attention as soon as it occurred and handle the situation in the usual manner. No matter what the source of your fear, mindfulness is the

118

cure. Observe the fear exactly as it is. Don't cling to it. Just watch it rising and growing. Study its effect. See how it makes you feel and how it affects your body. When you find yourself in the grip of horror fantasies, simply observe those mindfully. Watch the pictures as pictures. See memories as memories. Observe the emotional reactions that come along and know them for what they are. Stand aside from the process and don't get involved. Treat the whole dynamic as if you were an interested bystander. Most important, don't fight the situation. Don't try to repress the memories or the feelings or the fantasies. Just step out of the way and let the whole mess bubble up and flow past. It can't hurt you. It is just memory. It is only fantasy. It is nothing but fear.

When you let fear run its course in the arena of conscious attention, it won't sink back into the unconscious. It won't come back to haunt you later. It will be gone for good.

## PROBLEM 8—*Agitation*

Restlessness is often a cover-up for some deeper experience taking place in the unconscious. We humans are great at repressing things. Rather than confronting some unpleasant thought we experience, we try to bury it. We won't have to deal with the issue. Unfortunately, we usually don't succeed, at least not fully. We hide the thought, but the mental energy we use to cover it up sits there and boils. The result is that sense of unease which we call agitation or restlessness. There is nothing you can put your finger on. But you don't feel at ease. You can't relax. When this uncomfortable state arises in meditation, just observe it. Don't let it rule you. Don't jump up and run off. And don't struggle with it and try to make it go away. Just let it be there and watch it closely. Then the repressed material will eventually surface and you will find out what you have been worrying about.

The unpleasant experience that you have been trying to avoid could be almost anything: guilt, greed, or other problems. It could be low-grade pain or subtle sickness or approaching illness. Whatever it is, let it arise and look at it mindfully. If you just sit still and observe your agitation, it will eventually pass. Sitting through restlessness is a little breakthrough in your meditation career. It will teach you a lot. You will find that agitation is actually rather a superficial mental state. It is inherently ephemeral. It comes and it goes. It has no real grip on you at all.

PROBLEM 9—*Trying Too Hard*

Advanced meditators are generally found to be pretty jovial people. They possess one of the  most valuable of all human treasures, a sense of humor. It is not the superficial witty repartee of the talk show host. It is a real sense of humor. They can laugh at their own human failures. They can chuckle at personal disasters. Beginners in meditation are often much too serious for their own good. It is important to learn to loosen up in your session, to relax in your meditation. You need to learn to watch objectively whatever happens. You can't do that if you are tensed and striving, taking it all so very, very seriously. New meditators are often overly eager for results. They are full of enormous and inflated expectations. They jump right in and expect incredible results in no time flat. They push. They tense. They sweat and strain, and it is all so terribly, terribly grim and solemn. This state of tension is the antithesis of mindfulness. Naturally, they achieve little. Then they decide that this meditation is not so exciting after all. It did not give them what they wanted. They chuck it aside. It should be pointed out that you learn about meditation only by meditating. You learn what meditation is all about and where it leads only through direct experience of the thing itself. Therefore the beginner does not know where he is headed because he has developed little sense of where his practice is leading.

The novice's expectation is inherently unrealistic and uninformed. As a newcomer to meditation, he or she would expect all the wrong things, and those expectations do you no good at all. They get in the way. Trying too hard leads to rigidity and unhappiness, to guilt and self-condemnation. When you are trying too hard, your effort becomes mechanical and that defeats mindfulness before it even gets started. You are well-advised to drop all that. Drop your expectations and straining. Simply meditate with a steady and balanced effort. Enjoy your meditation and don't load yourself down with sweat and struggles. Just be mindful. The meditation itself will take care of the future.

## PROBLEM 10—*Discouragement*

The upshot of pushing too hard is frustration. You are in a state of tension. You get nowhere. You realize that you are not making the progress you expected, so you get discouraged. You feel like a failure. It is all a very natural cycle, but a totally avoidable one. Striving after unrealistic expectations is the source. Nevertheless, it is a common enough syndrome and, in spite of all the best advice, you may find it happening to you. There is a solution. If you find yourself discouraged, just observe your state of mind clearly. Don't add anything to it. Just watch it. A sense of failure is only another ephemeral emotional reaction. If you get involved, it feeds on your energy and it grows. If you simply stand aside and watch it, it passes away.

If you are discouraged over your perceived failure in meditation, that is especially easy to deal with. You feel you have failed in your practice. You have failed to be mindful. Simply become mindful of that sense of failure. You have just reestablished your mindfulness with that single step. The reason for your sense of failure is nothing but a memory. There is no such thing as failure in meditation. There are setbacks and difficulties. But there is no failure unless you give up entirely. Even if you have spent twenty solid years getting nowhere, you can be mindful at any second you choose to do so. It is your decision. Regretting is only one more way of being unmindful. The instant that you realize that you have been unmindful, that realization itself is an act of mindfulness. So continue the process. Don't get sidetracked by an emotional reaction.

PROBLEM 11—*Resistance to Meditation*

There are times when you don't feel like meditating. The very idea seems obnoxious. Missing a single practice session is scarcely important, but it very easily becomes a habit. It is wiser to push on through the resistance. Go sit anyway. Observe this feeling of aversion. In most cases it is a passing emotion, a flash in the pan that will evaporate right in front of your eyes. Five minutes after you sit down it is gone. In other cases it is due to some sour mood that day, and it lasts longer. Still, it does pass. And it is better to get rid of it in twenty or thirty minutes of meditation than to carry it around with you and let it ruin the rest of your day. At other times, resistance may be due to some difficulty you are having with the practice itself. You may or may not know what that difficulty is. If the problem is known, handle it by one of the techniques given in this book. Once the problem is gone, resistance will be gone. If the problem is unknown, then you are going to have to tough it out. Just sit through the resistance and observe it mindfully. It will pass. Then the problem causing it will probably bubble up in its wake, and you can deal with that.

If resistance to meditation is a common feature of your practice, then you should suspect some subtle error in your basic attitude. Meditation is not a ritual conducted in a particular posture. It is not a painful exercise, or period of enforced boredom. And it is not a grim, solemn obligation. Meditation is mindfulness. It is a new way of seeing and it is a form of play. Meditation is your friend. Come to regard it as such and resistance will disappear like smoke on a summer breeze.

If you try all these possibilities and the resistance remains, then there may be a problem. There can be certain metaphysical snags that a meditator runs into which go far beyond the scope of this book. It is not common for new meditators to hit these, but it can happen. Don't give up. Go and get help. Seek out qualified teachers of the Vipassana style of meditation and ask them to help you resolve the situation. Such people exist for exactly that purpose.

PROBLEM 12—*Stupor or Dullness*

We have already discussed the sinking mind phenomenon. But there is a special route to that state you should watch out for. Mental dullness can result as an unwanted by-product of deepening concentration. As your relaxation deepens, muscles loosen and nerve transmissions change. This produces a very calm and light feeling in the body. You feel very still and somewhat divorced from the body. This is good, nicely centered on the breath. As it continues, however, the pleasant feelings intensify and they distract your attention from the breath. You start to really enjoy the state and your mindfulness goes way down. Your attention winds up scattered, drifting listlessly through vague clouds of bliss. The result is a very unmindful state, sort of an ecstatic stupor. The cure, of course, is mindfulness. Mindfully observe these phenomena and they will dissipate. When blissful feelings arise accept them. There is no need to avoid them, but don't get wrapped up in them. They are physical feelings, so treat them as such. Observe feelings as feelings. Observe dullness as dullness. Watch them rise and watch them pass. Don't get involved.

You will have problems in meditation. Everybody does. You can treat them as terrible torments, or as challenges to be overcome. If you regard them as burdens, your suffering will only increase. If you regard them as opportunities to learn and to grow, your spiritual prospects are unlimited.

# CHAPTER 11

# DEALING WITH DISTRACTIONS I

At some time, every meditator encounters distractions during practice, and methods are needed to deal with them. Many useful stratagems have been devised to get you back on the track more quickly than trying to push your way through by sheer force of will. Concentration and mindfulness go hand-in-hand. Each one complements the other. If either one is weak, the other will eventually be affected. Bad days are usually characterized by poor concentration. Your mind just keeps floating around. You need a method of reestablishing your concentration, even in the face of mental adversity. Luckily, you have it. In fact, you can choose from an array of traditional practical maneuvers.

MANEUVER 1—*Time Gauging*

The first technique has been covered in an earlier chapter. A distraction has pulled you away from the breath, and you suddenly realize that you've been daydreaming. The trick is to pull all the way out of whatever has captured you, to break its hold on you completely so you can go back to the breath with full attention. You do this by gauging the length of time that you were distracted. This is not a precise calculation. You don't need a precise figure, just a rough estimate. You can figure it in minutes, or by idea significance. Just say to yourself, "Okay, I have been distracted for about two minutes," or "since the dog started barking," or "since I started thinking about money." When you first start practicing this technique, you will do it by talking to yourself. Once the habit is well-established, you can drop that, and the action becomes wordless and very quick. The whole idea, remember, is to pull out of the distraction and get back to the breath. You pull out of the thought by making it the object of inspection just long enough to glean from it a rough approximation of its duration. The interval itself is not important. Once you are free of the distraction, drop the whole thing and go back to the breath. Do not get hung up in the estimate.

## MANEUVER 2—*Deep Breaths*

When your mind is wild and agitated, you can often reestablish mindfulness with a few quick deep breaths. Pull the air in strongly and let it out the same way. This increases the sensation inside the nostrils and makes it easier to focus. Make a strong act of will and apply some force to your attention. Concentration can be forced into growth, so you will probably find your full attention settling nicely back on the breath.

## MANEUVER 3—*Counting*

Counting the breaths as they pass is a highly traditional procedure. Some schools of practice teach this activity as their primary tactic. Vipassana uses it as an auxiliary technique for reestablishing mindfulness and for strengthening concentration. As we discussed in Chapter 5, you can count breaths in a number of different ways. Remember to keep your attention on the breath. You will probably notice a change after you have done your counting. The breath slows down, or it becomes very light and refined. This is a physiological signal that concentration has become well-established. At this point, the breath is usually so light or so fast and gentle that you can't clearly distinguish the inhalation from the exhalation. They seem to blend into each other. You can then count both of them as a single cycle. Continue your counting process, but only up to a count of five, covering the same five-breath sequence, then start over. When counting becomes a bother, go on to the next step. Drop the numbers and forget about the concepts of inhalation and exhalation. Just dive right in to the pure sensation of breathing. Inhalation blends into exhalation. One breath blends into the next in a never-ending cycle of pure, smooth flow.

MANEUVER 4—*The In-Out Method*

This is an alternative to counting, and it functions in much the same manner. Just direct your attention to the breath and mentally tag each cycle with the words, "Inhalation...exhalation," or "In...out." Continue the process until you no longer need these concepts, and then throw them away.

MANEUVER 5—*Canceling One Thought With Another*

Some thoughts just won't go away. We humans are obsessional beings. It's one of our biggest problems. We tend to lock onto things like sexual fantasies and worries and ambitions. We feed those thought complexes over years of time and give them plenty of exercise by playing with them in every spare moment. Then when we sit down to meditate, we order them to go away and leave us alone. It is scarcely surprising that they don't obey. Persistent thoughts like these require a direct approach, a full-scale frontal attack.

Buddhist psychology has developed a distinct system of classification. Rather than dividing thoughts into classes like "good" and "bad," Buddhist thinkers prefer to regard them as "skillful" versus "unskillful." An unskillful thought is one connected with greed, hatred, or delusion. These are the thoughts that the mind most easily builds into obsessions. They are unskillful in the sense that they lead you away from the goal of Liberation. Skillful thoughts, on the other hand, are those connected with generosity, compassion, and wisdom. They are skillful in the sense that they may be used as specific remedies for unskillful thoughts, and thus can assist you toward Liberation.

You cannot condition Liberation. It is not a state built out of thoughts. Nor can you condition the personal qualities that Liberation produces. Thoughts of benevolence can produce a semblance of benevolence, but it's not the real item. It will break down under pressure. Thoughts of compassion produce only superficial compassion. Therefore, these skillful thoughts will not, in themselves, free you from the trap. They are skillful only if applied as antidotes to the poison of unskillful thoughts. Thoughts of generosity can temporarily cancel greed. They kick it under the rug long enough for mindfulness to do its work unhindered. Then, when mindfulness has penetrated to the roots of the ego process, greed evaporates and true generosity arises.

This principle can be used on a day-to-day basis in your own meditation. If a particular sort of obsession is troubling you, you can cancel it out by generating its opposite. Here is an example: If you absolutely hate Charlie, and his scowling face keeps popping into your mind, try directing a stream of love and friendliness toward Charlie. You probably will get rid of the immediate mental image. Then you can get on with the job of meditation.

Sometimes this tactic alone doesn't work. The obsession is

simply too strong. In this case you've got to weaken its hold on you somewhat before you can successfully balance it out. Here is where guilt, one of man's most misbegotten emotions, finally serves a purpose. Take a good strong look at the emotional response you are trying to get rid of. Actually ponder it. See how it makes you feel. Look at what it is doing to your life, your happiness, your health, and your relationships. Try to see how it makes you appear to others. Look at the way it is hindering your progress toward Liberation. The Pali scriptures urge you to do this very thoroughly indeed. They advise you to work up the same sense of disgust and humiliation that you would feel if you were forced to walk around with the carcass of a dead and decaying animal tied around your neck. Real loathing is what you are after. This step may end the problem all by itself. If it doesn't, then balance out the lingering remainder of the obsession by once again generating its opposite emotion.

Thoughts of greed cover everything connected with desire, from outright avarice for material gain, all the way to a subtle need to be respected as a moral person. Thoughts of hatred run the gamut from pettiness to murderous rage. Delusion covers everything from daydreaming to actual hallucinations. Generosity cancels greed. Benevolence and compassion cancel hatred. You can find a specific antidote for any troubling thought if you just think about it awhile.

## MANEUVER 6—*Recalling Your Purpose*

There are times when things pop into your mind, apparently at random. Words, phrases, or whole sentences jump up out of the unconscious for no discernible reason. Objects appear. Pictures flash on and off. This is an unsettling experience. Your mind feels like a flag flapping in a stiff wind. It washes back and forth like waves in the ocean. Often, at times like this, it is enough just to remember why you are there. You can say to yourself, "I'm not sitting here just to waste my time with these thoughts. I'm here to focus my mind on the breath, which is universal and common to all living beings." Sometimes your mind will settle down, even before you complete this recitation. Other times you may have to repeat it several times before you refocus on the breath.

These techniques can be used singly, or in combinations. Properly employed, they constitute quite an effective arsenal for your battle against the monkey mind.

CHAPTER 12

# DEALING WITH DISTRACTIONS II

So there you are, meditating beautifully. Your body is totally immobile, and your mind is totally still. You just glide right along following the flow of the breath, in, out, in, out...calm, serene, and concentrated. Everything is perfect. And then, all of a sudden, something totally different pops into your mind: "I sure wish I had an ice cream cone." That's a distraction, obviously. That's not what you are supposed to be doing. You notice that, and you drag yourself back to the breath, back to the smooth flow, in, out, in... And then: "Did I ever pay that gas bill?" Another distraction. You notice that one, and you haul yourself back to the breath. In, out, in, out, in... "That new science fiction movie is out. Maybe I can go see it Tuesday night. No, not Tuesday, got too much to do on Wednesday. Thursday's better..." Another distraction. You pull yourself out of that one, and back you go to the breath, except that you never quite get there, because before you do, that little voice in your head says, "My back is killing me." And on and on it goes, distraction after distraction, seemingly without end.

What a bother. But this is what it is all about. These distractions are actually the whole point. The key is to learn to deal with these things. Learning to notice them without being trapped in them. That's what we are here for. This mental wandering is unpleasant, to be sure. But it is the normal mode of operation of your mind. Don't think of it as the enemy. It is just the simple reality. And if you want to change something, the first thing you have to do is to see it the way it is.

When you first sit down to concentrate on the breath, you will be struck by how incredibly busy the mind actually is. It jumps and jibbers. It veers and bucks. It chases itself around in constant circles. It chatters. It thinks. It fantasizes and daydreams. Don't be upset about that. It's natural. When your mind wanders from the subject of meditation, just observe the distraction mindfully.

When we speak of a distraction in Insight meditation, we are speaking of any preoccupation that pulls the attention off the breath. This brings up a new, major rule for your meditation: When any mental state arises strongly enough to distract you from the object of meditation, switch your attention to the distraction briefly. Make the distraction a temporary object of meditation. Please note the word *temporary*. It's quite important. We are not advising that you switch horses in midstream. We do not expect you to adopt a whole new object of meditation every three seconds. The breath will always remain your primary focus. You switch your attention to the distraction only long enough to notice certain specific things about it. What is it? How strong is it? And, how long does it last?

As soon as you have wordlessly answered these questions, you are through with your examination of that distraction, and you return your attention to the breath. Here again, please note the operant term, *wordlessly*. These questions are not an invitation to more mental chatter. That would be moving you in the wrong direction, toward more thinking. We want you to move away from thinking, back to a direct, wordless, and non-conceptual experience of the breath. These questions are designed to free you from the distraction and give you insight into its nature, not to get you more thoroughly stuck in it. They will tune you in to what is distracting you and help you get rid of it—all in one step.

Here is the problem: When a distraction, or any mental state, arises in the mind, it blossoms forth first in the unconscious. Only a moment later does it rise to the conscious mind. That split-second difference is quite important, because it is time enough for grasping to occur. Grasping occurs almost instantaneously, and it takes place first in the unconscious. Thus, by the time the grasping rises to the level of conscious recognition, we have already begun to lock on to it. It is quite natural for us to simply continue that process, getting more and more tightly stuck in the distraction as we continue to view it. We are, by this time, quite definitely thinking the thought, rather than just viewing it with bare attention. The whole sequence takes place in a flash. This presents us with a problem. By the time we become consciously aware of a distraction, we are already, in a sense, stuck in it. Our three questions, "What is it? How strong is it? And, how long does it last?" are a clever remedy for this particular malady. In order to answer these questions, we must ascertain the quality of the distraction. To do that, we must divorce ourselves from it, take a mental step back from it, disengage from it, and view it objectively. We must stop thinking the thought or feeling the feeling in order to view it as an object of inspection. This very process is an exercise in *mindfulness,* uninvolved, detached awareness. The hold of the distraction is thus broken, and mindfulness is back in control. At this point, mindfulness makes a smooth transition back to its primary focus and we return to the breath.

When you first begin to practice this technique, you will probably have do it with words. You will ask your questions in words, and get answers in words. It won't be long, how-ever, before you can dispense with the formality of words altogether. Once the mental habits are in place, you simply note the distraction, note the qualities of the distraction, and return to the breath. It's a totally non-conceptual process, and it's very quick. The distraction itself can be anything: a sound, a sensation, an emotion, a fantasy, any-thing at all. Whatever it is, don't try to repress it. Don't try to force it out of your mind. There's no need for that. Just observe it mindfully with bare attention. Examine the dis-traction wordlessly and it will pass away by itself. You will find your attention drifting effortlessly back to the breath. And do not condemn yourself for having been distracted. Distractions are natural. They come and they go.

Despite this piece of sage counsel, you're going to find yourself condemning anyway. That's natural too. Just observe the process of condemnation as another distraction, and then return to the breath.

Watch the sequence of events: Breathing. Breathing. Distracting thought arises. Frustration arising over the dis-tracting thought. You condemn yourself for being distracted. You notice the self-condemnation. You return to the breathing. Breathing. Breathing. It's really a very natural, smooth-flowing cycle, if you do it correctly. The trick, of course, is patience. If you can learn to observe these distrac-tions without getting involved, it's all very easy. You just glide through the distraction and your attention returns to the breath quite easily. Of course, the very same distraction may pop up a moment later. If it does, just observe that mindfully. If you are dealing with an old, established thought pattern, this can go on happening for quite a while, sometimes years. Don't get upset. This too is natural. Just

observe the distraction and return to the breath. Don't fight
with these distracting thoughts. Don't strain or struggle. It's
a waste. Every bit of energy that you apply to that resistance
goes into the thought complex and makes it all the stronger.
So don't try to force such thoughts out of your mind. It's a
battle you can never win. Just observe the distraction mindfully and it will eventually go away. It's very strange, but the
more bare attention you pay to such disturbances, the weaker
they get. Observe them long enough and often enough with
bare attention and they fade away forever. Fight with them
and they gain strength. Watch them with detachment and
they wither.

Mindfulness is a function that disarms distractions, in the
same way that a munitions expert might defuse a bomb.
Weak distractions are disarmed by a single glance. Shine the
light of awareness on them and they evaporate instantly,
never to return. Deep-seated, habitual thought patterns
require constant mindfulness repeatedly applied over whatever time period it takes to break their hold. Distractions are
really paper tigers. They have no power of their own. They
need to be fed constantly, or else they die. If you refuse to
feed them by your own fear, anger, and greed, they fade.

Mindfulness is the most important aspect of meditation. It
is the primary thing that you are trying to cultivate. So
there is really no need at all to struggle against distractions.
The crucial thing is to be mindful of what is occurring, not
to control what is occurring. Remember, concentration is a
tool. It is secondary to bare attention. From the point of
view of mindfulness, there is really no such thing as a distraction. Whatever arises in the mind is viewed as just one more
opportunity to cultivate mindfulness. Breath, remember, is
an arbitrary focus, and it is used as our primary object of

attention. Distractions are used as secondary objects of attention. They are certainly as much a part of reality as breath. It actually makes rather little difference what the object of mindfulness is. You can be mindful of the breath, or you can be mindful of the distraction. You can be mindful of the fact that your mind is still, and your concentration is strong, or you can be mindful of the fact that your concentration is in ribbons and your mind is in an absolute shambles. It's all mindfulness. Just maintain that mindfulness and concentration eventually will follow.

The purpose of meditation is not to concentrate on the breath, without interruption, forever. That by itself would be a useless goal. The purpose of meditation is not to achieve a perfectly still and serene mind. Although a lovely state, it doesn't lead to liberation by itself. The purpose of meditation is to achieve uninterrupted mindfulness. Mindfulness, and only mindfulness, produces Enlightenment.

Distractions come in all sizes, shapes and flavors. Buddhist philosophy has organized them into categories. One of them is the category of hindrances. They are called hindrances because they block your development of both components of meditation, mindfulness and concentration. A bit of caution on this term: The word "hindrances" carries a negative connotation, and indeed these are states of mind we want to eradicate. That does not mean, however, that they are to be repressed, avoided, or condemned.

Let's use greed as an example. We wish to avoid prolonging any state of greed that arises, because a continuation of that state leads to bondage and sorrow. That does not mean we try to toss the thought out of the mind when it appears. We simply refuse to encourage it to stay. We let it come, and we let it go. When greed is first observed with bare attention, no value judgments are made. We simply stand back and watch it arise. The whole dynamic of greed from start to finish is simply observed in this way. We don't help it, or hinder it, or interfere with it in the slightest. It stays as long as it stays. And we learn as much about it as we can while it is there. We watch what greed does. We watch how it troubles us, and how it burdens others. We notice how it keeps us perpetually unsatisfied, forever in a state of unfulfilled longing. From this first-hand experience, we ascertain at a gut level that greed is an unskillful way to run your life. There is nothing theoretical about this realization.

All of the hindrances are dealt with in the same way, and we will look at them here one by one.

*Desire:* Let us suppose you have been distracted by some nice experience in meditation. It could be a pleasant fantasy or a thought of pride. It might be a feeling of self-esteem. It might be a thought of love or even the physical sensation of bliss that comes with the meditation experience itself. Whatever it is, what follows is the state of desire—desire to obtain whatever you have been thinking about or desire to prolong the experience you are having. No matter what its nature, you should handle desire in the following manner. Notice the thought or sensation as it arises. Notice the mental state of desire which accompanies it as a separate thing. Notice the exact extent or degree of that desire. Then notice how long it lasts and when it finally disappears. When you have done that, return your attention to breathing.

*Aversion:* Suppose that you have been distracted by some negative experience. It could be something you fear or some nagging worry. It might be guilt or depression or pain.

Whatever the actual substance of the thought or sensation, you find yourself rejecting or repressing—trying to avoid it, resist it, or deny it. The handling here is essentially the same. Watch the arising of the thought or sensation. Notice the state of rejection that comes with it. Gauge the extent or degree of that rejection. See how long it lasts and when it fades away. Then return your attention to your breath.

*Lethargy:* Lethargy comes in various grades and intensities, ranging from slight drowsiness to total torpor. We are talking about a mental state here, not a physical one. Sleepiness or physical fatigue is something quite different and, in the Buddhist system of classification, it would be categorized as a physical feeling. Mental lethargy is closely related to aversion in that it is one of the mind's clever little ways of avoiding those issues it finds unpleasant. Lethargy is a sort of turn-off of the mental apparatus, a dulling of sensory and cognitive acuity. It is an enforced stupidity pretending to be sleep. This can be a tough one to deal with, because its presence is directly contrary to the employment of mindfulness. Lethargy is nearly the reverse of mindfulness. Nevertheless, mindfulness is the cure for this hindrance, too, and the handling is the same. Note the state of drowsiness when it arises, and note its extent or degree. Note when it arises, how long it lasts, and when it passes away. The only thing special here is the importance of catching the phenomenon early. You have got to get it right at its conception and apply liberal doses of pure awareness right away. If you let it get a start, its growth will probably outpace your mindfulness power. When lethargy wins, the result is the sinking mind, or even sleep.

*Agitation:* States of restlessness and worry are expressions of mental agitation. Your mind keeps darting around, refusing to settle on any one thing. You may keep running over and over the same issues. But even here, an unsettled feeling is the predominant component. The mind refuses to settle anywhere. It jumps around constantly. The cure for this condition is the same basic sequence. Restlessness imparts a certain feeling to consciousness. You might call it a flavor or texture. Whatever you call it, that unsettled feeling is there as a definable characteristic. Look for it. Once you have spotted it, note how much of it is present. Note when it arises. Watch how long it lasts, and see when it fades away. Then return your attention to the breath.

*Doubt:* Doubt has its own distinct feeling in consciousness. The Pali texts describe it very nicely. It's the feeling of a man stumbling through a desert and arriving at an unmarked crossroad. Which road should he take? There is no way to tell. So he just stands there vacillating. One of the common forms this takes in meditation is an inner dialogue something like this: "What am I doing just sitting like this? Am I really getting anything out of this at all? Oh! Sure I am. This is good for me. The book said so. No, that is crazy. This is a waste of time. No, I won't give up. I said I was going to do this, and I am going to do it. Or am I just being stubborn? I don't know. I just don't know." Don't get stuck in this trap. It is just another hindrance. Another of the mind's little smoke screens to keep you from actually becoming aware of what is happening. To handle doubt, simply become aware of this mental state of wavering as an object of inspection. Don't be trapped in it. Back out of it and look at it. See how strong it is. See when it comes and how long it lasts. Then watch it fade away, and go back to the breathing.

This is the general pattern you will use on any distraction that arises. By distraction, remember we mean any mental state that arises to impede your meditation. Some of these are quite subtle. It is useful to list some of the possibilities. The negative states are pretty easy to spot: insecurity, fear, anger, depression, irritation, and frustration.

Craving and desire are a bit more difficult to spot because they can apply to things we normally regard as virtuous or noble. You can experience the desire to perfect yourself. You can feel craving for greater virtue. You can even develop an attachment to the bliss of the meditation experience itself. It is a bit hard to detach yourself from such altruistic feelings. In the end, though, it is just more greed. It is a desire for gratification and a clever way of ignoring the present-time reality.

Trickiest of all, however, are those really positive mental states that come creeping into your meditation. Happiness, peace, inner contentment, sympathy, and compassion for all beings everywhere. These mental states are so sweet and so benevolent that you can scarcely bear to pry yourself loose from them. It makes you feel like a traitor to mankind. There is no need to feel this way. We are not advising you to reject these states of mind or to become heartless robots. We merely want you to see them for what they are. They are mental states. They come, and they go. They arise, and they pass away. As you continue your meditation, these states will arise more often. The trick is not to become attached to them. Just see each one as it comes up. See what it is, how strong it is, and how long it lasts. Then watch it drift away. It is all just more of the passing show of your own mental universe.

Just as breathing comes in stages, so do the mental states. Every breath has a beginning, a middle, and an end. Every mental state has a birth, a growth, and a decay. You should strive to see these stages clearly. This is no easy thing to do, however. As we have already noted, every thought and sensation begins first in the unconscious region of the mind and only later rises to consciousness. We generally become aware of such things only after they have arisen in the conscious realm and stayed there for some time. Indeed we usually become aware of distractions only when they have released their hold on us and are already on their way out. It is at this point that we are struck with that sudden realization that we have been somewhere, daydreaming, fantasizing, or whatever. Quite obviously this is far too late in the chain of events. We may call this phenomenon catching the lion by his tail, and it is an unskillful thing to do. Like confronting a dangerous beast, we must approach mental states head-on. Patiently, we will learn to recognize them as they arise from progressively deeper levels of our conscious mind.

Since mental states arise first in the unconscious, to catch the arising of the mental state, you've got to extend your awareness down into this unconscious area. That is difficult, because you can't see what is going on down there, at least not in the same way you see a conscious thought. But you can learn to get a vague sense of movement and to operate by a sort of mental sense of touch. This comes with practice, and the ability is another of the effects of the deep calm of concentration. Concentration slows down the arising of these mental states and gives you time to feel each one arising out of the unconscious even before you see it in consciousness. Concentration helps you to extend your awareness down into that boiling darkness where thought and sensation begin.

As your concentration deepens, you gain the ability to see

thoughts and sensations arising slowly, like separate bubbles, each distinct and with spaces between them. They bubble up in slow motion out of the unconscious. They stay a while in the conscious mind and then they drift away.

The application of awareness to mental states is a precision operation. This is particularly true of feelings or sensation. It is very easy to overreach the sensation. That is, to add something to it above and beyond what is really there. It is equally easy to fall short of sensation, to get part of it but not all. The ideal that you are striving for is to experience each mental state fully, exactly the way it is, adding nothing to it and not missing any part of it. Let us use pain in the leg as an example. What is actually there is a pure flowing sensation. It changes constantly, never the same from one moment to the next. It moves from one location to another, and its intensity surges up and down. Pain is not a thing. It is an event. There should be no concepts tacked on to it and none associated with it. A pure unobstructed awareness of this event will experience it simply as a flowing pattern of energy and nothing more. No thought and no rejection. Just energy.

Early on in our practice of meditation, we need to rethink our underlying assumptions regarding conceptualization. For most of us, we have earned high marks in school and in life for our ability to manipulate mental phenomena, or concepts, logically. Our careers, much of our success in everyday life, our happy relationships, we view as largely the result of our successful manipulation of concepts. In developing mindfulness, however, we temporarily suspend the conceptualization process and focus on the pure nature of mental phenomena. During meditation we are seeking to experience the mind at the pre-conceptual level.

But the human mind conceptualizes such occurrences as pain. You find yourself thinking of it as "the pain." That is a concept. It is a label, something added to the sensation itself. You find yourself building a mental image, a picture of the pain, seeing it as a shape. You may see a diagram of the leg with the pain outlined in some lovely color. This is very creative and terribly entertaining, but not what we want. Those are concepts tacked on to the living reality. Most likely, you will probably find yourself thinking: "I have a pain in my leg." "I" is a concept. It is something extra added to the pure experience.

When you introduce "I" into the process, you are building a conceptual gap between the reality and the awareness viewing that reality. Thoughts such as "me," "my," or "mine" have no place in direct awareness. They are extraneous addenda, and insidious ones at that. When you bring "me" into the picture, you are identifying with the pain. That simply adds emphasis to it. If you leave "I" out of the operation, pain is not painful. It is just a pure surging energy flow. It can even be beautiful. If you find "I" insinuating itself in your experience of pain or indeed any other sensation, then just observe that mindfully. Pay bare attention to the phenomenon of personal identification with pain.

The general idea, however, is almost too simple. You want to really see each sensation, whether it is pain, bliss, or boredom. You want to experience that thing fully in its natural and unadulterated form. There is only one way to do this. Your timing has to be precise. Your awareness of each sensation must coordinate exactly with the arising of that sensation. If you catch it just a bit too late, you miss the beginning. You won't get all of it. If you hang on to any sensation past the time when it has faded away, then what you are holding onto is a memory. The thing itself is gone, and by holding onto that memory, you miss the arising of the next sensation. It is a very delicate operation. You've got to cruise along right here in present time, picking things up and letting things drop with no delays whatsoever. It takes a very light touch. Your relation to sensation should never be one of past or future but always of the simple and immediate now.

The human mind seeks to conceptualize phenomena, and it has developed a host of clever ways to do so. Every simple sensation will trigger a burst of conceptual thinking if you give the mind its way. Let us take hearing, for example. You are sitting in meditation and somebody in the next room drops a dish. The sounds strike your ear. Instantly you see a picture of that other room. You probably see a person dropping a dish, too. If this is a familiar environment, say your own home, you probably will have a 3-D technicolor mind movie of who did the dropping and which dish was dropped. This whole sequence presents itself to consciousness instantly. It just jumps out of the unconscious so bright and clear and compelling that it shoves everything else out of sight. What happens to the original sensation, the pure experience of hearing? It gets lost in the shuffle, completely overwhelmed and forgotten. We miss reality. We enter a world of fantasy.

Here is another example: You are sitting in meditation and a sound strikes your ear. It is just an indistinct noise, sort of a muffled crunch; it could be anything. What happens next will probably be something like this. "What was that? Who did that? Where did that come from? How far away was that? Is it dangerous?" And on and on you go, getting no answers but your fantasy projection. Conceptualization is an insidiously clever process. It creeps into your experience, and it simply takes over. When you hear a sound in meditation, pay bare attention to the experience of hearing. That and that only. What is really happening is so utterly simple that we can and do miss it altogether. Sound waves are striking the ear in a certain unique pattern. Those waves are being translated into electrical impulses within the brain and those impulses present a sound pattern to consciousness. That is all. No pictures. No mind movies. No concepts. No interior dialogues about the question. Just noise. Reality is elegantly simple and unadorned. When you hear a sound, be mindful of the process of hearing. Everything else is just added chatter. Drop it. This same rule applies to every sensation, every emotion, every experience you may have. Look closely at your own experience. Dig down through the layers of mental bric-a-brac and see what is really there. You will be amazed how simple it is, and how beautiful.

There are times when a number of sensations may arise at once. You might have a thought of fear, a squeezing in the stomach, an aching back and an itch on your left earlobe, all at the same time. Don't sit there in a quandary. Don't keep switching back and forth or wondering what to pick. One of them will be strongest. Just open yourself up, and the most insistent of these phenomena will intrude itself and demand your attention. So give it some attention just long enough to see it fade away. Then return to your breathing. If another one intrudes itself, let it in. When it is done, return to the breathing.

This process can be carried too far, however. Don't sit there looking for things to be mindful of. Keep your mindfulness on the breath until something else steps in and pulls your attention away. When you feel that happening, don't fight it. Let your attention flow naturally over to the distraction, and keep it there until the distraction evaporates. Then return to breathing. Don't seek out other physical or mental phenomena. Just return to breathing. Let them come to you. There will be times when you drift off, of course. Even after long practice you find yourself suddenly waking up, realizing you have been off the track for some while. Don't get discouraged. Realize that you have been off the track for such and such a length of time and go back to the breath. There is no need for any negative reaction at all. The very act of realizing that you have been off the track is an active awareness. It is an exercise of pure mindfulness all by itself.

Mindfulness grows by the exercise of mindfulness. It is like exercising a muscle. Every time you work it, you pump it up just a little. You make it a little stronger. The very fact that you have felt that wake-up sensation means that you have just improved your mindfulness power. That means you win. Move back to the breathing without regret. However, the regret is a conditioned reflex, and it may come along anyway—another mental habit. If you find yourself getting frustrated, feeling discouraged, or condemning yourself, just observe that with bare attention. It is just another distraction. Give it some attention and watch it fade away, and return to the breath.

The rules we have just reviewed can and should be applied thoroughly to all of your mental states. You are going to find this an utterly ruthless injunction. It is the toughest job that you will ever undertake. You will find yourself relatively willing to apply this technique to certain parts of your experience, and you will find yourself totally unwilling to use it on the other parts.

Meditation is a bit like mental acid. It eats away slowly at whatever you put it on. We humans are very odd beings. We like the taste of certain poisons and we stubbornly continue to eat them even while they are killing us. Thoughts to which we are attached are poison. You will find yourself quite eager to dig some thoughts out by the roots while you jealously guard and cherish certain others. That is the human condition.

Vipassana meditation is not a game. Clear awareness is more than a pleasurable pastime. It is a road up and out of the quagmire in which we are all stuck, the swamp of our own desires and aversions. It is relatively easy to apply awareness to the nastier aspects of your existence. Once you have seen fear and depression evaporate under the hot, intense beacon of awareness, you will want to repeat that process. Those are the unpleasant mental states. They hurt. You want to get rid of those things because they bother you. It is a good deal harder to apply that same process to mental states which you cherish, like patriotism, or parental protectiveness or true love. But it is just as necessary. Positive attachments hold you in the mud just as assuredly as negative attachments. You may rise above the mud far enough to breathe a bit more easily if you practice Vipassana meditation with diligence. Vipassana meditation is the road to Nibbana. And from the reports of those who have toiled their way to that lofty goal, it is well worth every effort involved.

# CHAPTER 13

# MINDFULNESS (SATI)

Mindfulness is the English translation of the Pali word *Sati. Sati* is an activity. What exactly is that? There can be no precise answer, at least not in words. Words are devised by the symbolic levels of the mind and they describe those realities with which symbolic thinking deals. Mindfulness is pre-symbolic. It is not shackled to logic. Nevertheless, mindfulness can be experienced—rather easily—and it can be described, as long as you keep in mind that the words are only fingers pointing at the moon. They are not the thing itself. The actual experience lies beyond the words and above the symbols. Mindfulness could be described in completely different terms than will be used here and each description could still be correct.

Mindfulness is a subtle process that you are using at this very moment. The fact that this process lies above and beyond words does not make it unreal—quite the reverse. Mindfulness is the reality which gives rise to words—the words that follow are simply pale shadows of reality. So, it is important to understand that everything that follows here is analogy. It is not going to make perfect sense. It will always remain beyond verbal logic. But you can experience it. The meditation technique called Vipassana (Insight) that was introduced by the Buddha about twenty-five centuries ago is a set of mental activities specifically aimed at experiencing a state of uninterrupted mindfulness.

When you first become aware of something, there is a

fleeting instant of pure awareness just before you conceptualize the thing, before you identify it. That is a state of awareness. Ordinarily, this state is short-lived. It is that flashing split second just as you focus your eyes on the thing, just as you focus your mind on the thing, just before you objectify it, clamp down on it mentally and segregate it from the rest of existence. It takes place just before you start thinking about it—before your mind says, "Oh, it's a dog." That flowing, soft-focused moment of pure awareness is mindfulness. In that brief flashing mind-moment you experience a thing as an un-thing. You experience a softly flowing moment of pure experience that is interlocked with the rest of reality, not separate from it. Mindfulness is very much like what you see with your peripheral vision as opposed to the hard focus of normal or central vision. Yet this moment of soft, unfocused, awareness contains a very deep sort of knowing that is lost as soon as you focus your mind and objectify the object into a thing. In the process of ordinary perception, the mindfulness step is so fleeting as to be unobservable. We have developed the habit of squandering our attention on all the remaining steps, focusing on the perception, cognizing the perception, labeling it, and most of all, getting involved in a long string of symbolic thought about it. That original moment of mindfulness is rapidly passed over. It is the purpose of Vipassana meditation to train us to prolong that moment of awareness.

When this mindfulness is prolonged by using proper techniques, you find that this experience is profound and it changes your entire view of the universe. This state of perception has to be learned, however, and it takes regular practice. Once you learn the technique, you will find that mindfulness has many interesting aspects.

## THE CHARACTERISTICS OF MINDFULNESS

Mindfulness is mirror-thought. It reflects only what is presently happening and in exactly the way it is happening. There are no biases.

Mindfulness is non-judgmental observation. It is that ability of the mind to observe without criticism. With this ability, one sees things without condemnation or judgment. One is surprised by nothing. One simply takes a balanced interest in things exactly as they are in their natural states. One does not decide and does not judge. One just observes. Please note that when we say, "One does not decide and does not judge," what we mean is that the meditator observes experiences very much like a scientist observing an object under a microscope without any preconceived notions, only to see the object exactly as it is. In the same way the meditator notices impermanence, unsatisfactoriness and selflessness.

It is psychologically impossible for us to objectively observe what is going on within us if we do not at the same time accept the occurrence of our various states of mind. This is especially true with unpleasant states of mind. In order to observe our own fear, we must accept the fact that we are afraid. We can't examine our own depression without accepting it fully. The same is true for irritation and agitation, frustration and all those other uncomfortable emotional states. You can't examine something fully if you are busy rejecting its existence. Whatever experience we may be having, mindfulness just accepts it. It is simply another of life's occurrences, just another thing to be aware of. No pride, no shame, nothing personal at stake—what is there, is there.

Mindfulness is an impartial watchfulness. It does not take sides. It does not get hung up in what is perceived. It just perceives. Mindfulness does not get infatuated with the good mental states. It does not try to sidestep the bad mental states. There is no clinging to the pleasant, no fleeing from the unpleasant. Mindfulness treats all experiences equally, all thoughts equally, all feelings equally. Nothing is suppressed. Nothing is repressed. Mindfulness does not play favorites.

Mindfulness is non-conceptual awareness. Another English term for *Sati* is "bare attention." It is not thinking. It does not get involved with thought or concepts. It does not get hung up on ideas or opinions or memories. It just looks. Mindfulness registers experiences, but it does not compare them. It does not label them or categorize them. It just observes everything as if it was occurring for the first time. It is not analysis which is based on reflection and memory. It is, rather, the direct and immediate experiencing of whatever is happening, without the medium of thought. It comes before thought in the perceptual process.

Mindfulness is present-time awareness. It takes place in the here and now. It is the observance of what is happening right now, in the present moment. It stays forever in the present, perpetually on the crest of the ongoing wave of passing time. If you are remembering your second-grade teacher, that is memory. When you then become aware that you are remembering your second-grade teacher, that is mindfulness. If you then conceptualize the process and say to yourself, "Oh, I am remembering," that is thinking.

Mindfulness is non-egotistic alertness. It takes place without reference to self. With mindfulness one sees all phenomena without references to concepts like "me," "my," or "mine." For example, suppose there is pain in your left leg. Ordinary consciousness would say, "I have a pain." Using mindfulness, one would simply note the sensation as a sensation. One would not tack on that extra concept "I." Mindfulness stops one from adding anything to perception, or subtracting anything from it. One does not enhance anything. One does not emphasize anything. One just observes exactly what is there—without distortion.

Mindfulness is awareness of change. It is observing the passing flow of experience. It is watching things as they are changing. It is seeing the birth, growth, and maturity of all phenomena. It is watching phenomena decay and die. Mindfulness is watching things moment by moment, continuously. It is observing all phenomena—physical, mental, or emotional—whatever is presently taking place in the mind. One just sits back and watches the show. Mindfulness is the observance of the basic nature of each passing phenomenon. It is watching the thing arising and passing away. It is seeing how that thing makes us feel and how we react to it. It is observing how it affects others. In mindfulness, one is an unbiased observer whose sole job is to keep track of the constantly passing show of the universe within. *Please note that last point.* In mindfulness, one watches the universe within. The meditator who is developing mindfulness is not concerned with the external universe. It is there, but in meditation, one's field of study is one's own experience, one's thoughts, one's feelings, and one's perceptions. In meditation, one is one's own laboratory. The universe within has an enormous fund of information containing the reflection of the external world and much more. An examination of this material leads to total freedom.

Mindfulness is participatory observation. The meditator is both participant and observer at one and the same time. If one watches one's emotions or physical sensations, one is feeling them at that very same moment. Mindfulness is not an intellectual awareness. It is just awareness. The mirror-thought metaphor breaks down here. Mindfulness is objective, but it is not cold or unfeeling. It is the wakeful experience of life, an alert participation in the ongoing process of living.

Mindfulness is extremely difficult to define in words—not because it is complex, but because it is too simple and open. The same problem crops up in every area of human experience. The most basic concept is always the most difficult to pin down. Look at a dictionary and you will see a clear example. Long words generally have concise definitions, but for short basic words like "the" and "is," definitions can be a page long. And in physics, the most difficult functions to describe are the most basic—those that deal with the most fundamental realities of quantum mechanics. Mindfulness is a pre-symbolic function. You can play with word symbols all day long and you will never pin it down completely. We can never fully express what it is. However, we can say what it does.

## THREE FUNDAMENTAL ACTIVITIES

There are three fundamental activities of mindfulness. We can use these activities as functional definitions of the term: (a) mindfulness reminds us of what we are supposed to be doing; (b) it sees things as they really are; and (c) it sees the true nature of all phenomena. Let's examine these definitions in greater detail.

*(a) Mindfulness reminds you of what you are supposed to be doing.* In meditation, you put your attention on one item. When your mind wanders from this focus, it is mindfulness that reminds you that your mind is wandering and what you are supposed to be doing. It is mindfulness that brings your mind back to the object of meditation. All of

this occurs instantaneously and without internal dialogue. Mindfulness is not thinking. Repeated practice in meditation establishes this function as a mental habit which then carries over into the rest of your life. A serious meditator pays bare attention to occurrences all the time, day in, day out, whether formally sitting in meditation or not. This is a very lofty ideal towards which those who meditate may be working for a period of years or even decades. Our habit of getting stuck in thought is years old, and that habit will hang on in the most tenacious manner. The only way out is to be equally persistent in the cultivation of constant mindfulness. When mindfulness is present, you will notice when you become stuck in your thought patterns. It is that very noticing which allows you to back out of the thought process and free yourself from it. Mindfulness then returns your attention to its proper focus. If you are meditating at that moment, then your focus will be the formal object of meditation. If you are not in formal meditation, it will be just a pure application of bare attention itself, just a pure noticing of whatever comes up without getting involved—"Ah, this comes up...and now this, and now this...and now this."

Mindfulness is at one and the same time both bare attention itself and the function of reminding us to pay bare attention if we have ceased to do so. Bare attention is noticing. It reestablishes itself simply by noticing that it has not been present. As soon as you are noticing that you have not been noticing, then by definition you are noticing and then you are back again to paying bare attention.

Mindfulness creates its own distinct feeling in consciousness. It has a flavor—a light, clear, energetic flavor. By comparison, conscious thought is heavy, ponderous, and picky.

But here again, these are just words. Your own practice will show you the difference. Then you will probably come up with your own words and the words used here will become superfluous. Remember, practice is the thing.

*(b) Mindfulness sees things as they really are.* Mindfulness adds nothing to perception and it subtracts nothing. It distorts nothing. It is bare attention and just looks at whatever comes up. Conscious thought pastes things over our experience, loads us down with concepts and ideas, immerses us in a churning vortex of plans and worries, fears and fantasies. When mindful, you don't play that game. You just notice exactly what arises in the mind, then you notice the next thing. "Ah, this...and this...and now this." It is really very simple.

*(c) Mindfulness sees the true nature of all phenomena.* Mindfulness and only mindfulness can perceive that the three prime characteristics that Buddhism teaches are the deepest truths of existence. In Pali these three are called *Anicca* (impermanence), *Dukkha* (unsatisfactoriness), and *Anatta* (selflessness—the absence of a permanent, unchanging entity that we call Soul or Self). These truths are not presented in Buddhist teaching as dogmas demanding blind faith. The Buddhists feel that these truths are universal and self-evident to anyone who cares to investigate in a proper way. Mindfulness is that method of investigation. Mindfulness alone has the power to reveal the deepest level of reality available to human observation. At this level of inspection, one sees the following: (a) all conditioned things are inherently transitory; (b) every worldly thing is, in the end, unsatisfying; and (c) there are really no entities that are unchanging or permanent, only processes.

Mindfulness works like an electron microscope. That is, it

operates on so fine a level that one can actually directly perceive those realities which are at best theoretical constructs to the conscious thought process. Mindfulness actually sees the impermanent character of every perception. It sees the transitory and passing nature of everything that is perceived. It also sees the inherently unsatisfactory nature of all conditioned things. It sees that there is no sense grabbing onto any of these passing shows. Peace and happiness cannot be found that way. And finally, mindfulness sees the inherent selflessness of all phenomena. It sees the way that we have arbitrarily selected a certain bundle of perceptions, chopped them off from the rest of the surging flow of experience and then conceptualized them as separate, enduring entities. Mindfulness actually sees these things. It does not think about them, it sees them directly.

When it is fully developed, mindfulness sees these three attributes of existence directly, instantaneously, and without the intervening medium of conscious thought. In fact, even the attributes which we just covered are inherently unified. They don't really exist as separate items. They are purely the result of our struggle to take this fundamentally simple process called mindfulness and express it in the cumbersome and inadequate thought symbols of the conscious level. Mindfulness is a process, but it does not take place in steps. It is a holistic process that occurs as a unit: you notice your own lack of mindfulness; and that noticing itself is a result of mindfulness; and mindfulness is bare attention; and bare attention is noticing things exactly as they are without distortion; and the way they are is impermanent *(Anicca)*, unsatisfactory *(Dukkha)*, and selfless *(Anatta)*. It all takes place in the space of a few mind-moments. This does not mean, however, that you will instantly attain

Liberation (freedom from all human weaknesses) as a result of your first moment of mindfulness. Learning to integrate this material into your conscious life is quite another process. And learning to prolong this state of mindfulness is still another. They are joyous processes, however, and they are well worth the effort.

## MINDFULNESS (SATI) AND INSIGHT (VIPASSANA) MEDITATION

Mindfulness is the center of Vipassana meditation and the key to the whole process. It is both the goal of this meditation and the means to that end. You reach mindfulness by being ever more mindful. One other Pali word that is translated into English as mindfulness is *Appamada,* which means non-negligence or absence of madness. One who attends constantly to what is really going on in one's mind achieves the state of ultimate sanity.

The Pali term *Sati* also bears the connotation of remembering. It is not memory in the sense of ideas and pictures from the past, but rather clear, direct, wordless knowing of what is and what is not, of what is correct and what is incorrect, of what we are doing and how we should go about it. Mindfulness reminds the meditator to apply his attention to the proper object at the proper time and to exert precisely the amount of energy needed to do that job. When this energy is properly applied, the meditator stays constantly in a state of calm and alertness. As long as this condition is maintained, those mind-states called "hindrances" or "psychic irritants" cannot arise—there is no greed, no hatred, no lust or laziness. But we all are human and we all err. Most of us err repeatedly. Despite honest effort, the meditator lets his mindfulness slip now and then and he finds himself stuck in some regrettable, but normal, human failure. It is mindfulness that notices that change. And it is mindfulness that reminds him to apply the energy required to pull himself out. These slips happen over and over, but their frequency decreases with practice. Once mindfulness has pushed these mental defilements aside, more wholesome states of mind can take their place. Hatred makes way for loving-kindness, lust is replaced by detachment. It is mindfulness which notices this change, too, and which reminds the Vipassana meditator to maintain that extra little mental sharpness needed to retain these more desirable states of mind. Mindfulness makes possible the growth of wisdom and compassion. Without mindfulness they cannot develop to full maturity.

Deeply buried in the mind, there lies a mental mechanism which accepts what the mind perceives as beautiful and pleasant experiences and rejects those experiences which are perceived as ugly and painful. This mechanism gives rise to those states of mind which we are training ourselves to avoid – things like greed, lust, hatred, aversion, and jealousy. We choose to avoid these hindrances, not because they are evil in the normal sense of the word, but because they are compulsive; because they take the mind over and capture the attention completely; because they keep going round and round in tight little circles of thought; and because they seal us off from living reality.

These hindrances cannot arise when mindfulness is present. Mindfulness is attention to present time reality, and therefore, directly antithetical to the dazed state of mind which characterizes impediments. As meditators, it is only when we let our mindfulness slip that the deep mechanisms of our mind take over—grasping, clinging, and rejecting.

Then resistance emerges and obscures our awareness. We do not notice that the change is taking place—we are too busy with a thought of revenge, or greed, whatever it may be. While an untrained person will continue in this state indefinitely, a trained meditator will soon realize what is happening. It is mindfulness that notices the change. It is mindfulness that remembers the training received and that focuses our attention so that the confusion fades away. And it is mindfulness that then attempts to maintain itself indefinitely so that the resistance cannot arise again. Thus, mindfulness is the specific antidote for hindrances. It is both the cure and the preventive measure.

Fully developed mindfulness is a state of total non-attachment and utter absence of clinging to anything in the world. If we can maintain this state, no other means or device is needed to keep ourselves free of obstructions, to achieve liberation from our human weaknesses. Mindfulness is non-superficial awareness. It sees things deeply, down below the level of concepts and opinions. This sort of deep observation leads to total certainty, a complete absence of confusion. It manifests itself primarily as a constant and unwavering attention which never flags and never turns away.

This pure and unstained investigative awareness not only holds mental hindrances at bay, it lays bare their very mechanism and destroys them. Mindfulness neutralizes defilements in the mind. The result is a mind which remains unstained and invulnerable, completely unaffected by the ups and downs of life.

# CHAPTER 14

# MINDFULNESS VERSUS CONCENTRATION

Vipassana meditation is something of a mental balancing act. You are going to be cultivating two separate qualities of the mind—mindfulness and concentration. Ideally, these two work together as a team. They pull in tandem, so to speak. Therefore it is important to cultivate them side-by-side and in a balanced manner. If one of the factors is strengthened at the expense of the another, the balance of the mind is lost and meditation becomes impossible.

Concentration and mindfulness are distinctly different functions. They each have their role to play in meditation, and the relationship between them is definite and delicate. Concentration is often called one-pointedness of mind. It consists of forcing the mind to remain on one static point. Please note the word *force*. Concentration is pretty much a forced type of activity. It can be developed by force, by sheer unremitting willpower. And once developed, it retains some of that forced flavor. Mindfulness, on the other hand, is a delicate function leading to refined sensibilities. These two are partners in the job of meditation. Mindfulness is the sensitive one. He notices things. Concentration provides the power. He keeps the attention pinned down to one item. Ideally, mindfulness is in this relationship. Mindfulness picks the objects of attention, and notices when the attention has gone astray. Concentration does the actual work of holding the attention steady on that chosen object. If either of these partners is weak, your meditation goes astray.

Concentration could be defined as that faculty of the mind which focuses single-mindedly on one object without interruption. It must be emphasized that true concentration is a wholesome one-pointedness of mind. That is, the state is free from greed, hatred, and delusion. Unwholesome one-pointedness is also possible, but it will not lead to Liberation. You can be very single-minded in a state of lust. But that gets you nowhere. Uninterrupted focus on something that you hate does not help you at all. In fact, such unwholesome concentration is fairly short-lived even when it is achieved—especially when it is used to harm others. True concentration itself is free from such contaminants. It is a state in which the mind is gathered together and thus gains power and intensity. We might use the analogy of a lens. Parallel waves of sunlight falling on a piece of paper will do no more than warm the surface. But that same amount of light, when focused through a lens, falls on a single point and the paper bursts into flames. Concentration is the lens. It produces the burning intensity necessary to see into the deeper reaches of the mind. Mindfulness selects the object that the lens will focus on and looks through the lens to see what is there.

Concentration should be regarded as a tool. Like any tool, it can be used for good or for ill. A sharp knife can be used to create a beautiful carving or to harm someone. It is all up to the one who uses the knife. Concentration is similar. Properly used, it can assist you toward Liberation. But it can also be used in the service of the ego. It can operate in the framework of achievement and competition. You can use concentration to dominate others. You can use it to be selfish. The real problem is that concentration alone will not give you a perspective on yourself. It won't throw light on the basic problems of selfishness and the nature of suffering. It can be used to dig down into deep psychological states. But even then, the forces of egotism won't be understood. Only mindfulness can do that. If mindfulness is not there to look into the lens and see what has been uncovered, then it is all for nothing. Only mindfulness understands. Only mindfulness brings wisdom. Concentration has other limitations, too.

Really deep concentration can only take place under certain specific conditions. Buddhists go to a lot of trouble to build meditation halls and monasteries. Their main purpose is to create a physical environment free of distractions in which to learn this skill. No noise, no interruptions. Just as important, however, is the creation of a distraction-free emotional environment. The development of concentration will be blocked by the presence of certain mental states which we call the five hindrances. They are greed for sensual pleasure, hatred, mental lethargy, restlessness, and mental vacillation. We have examined these mental states more fully in Chapter 12.

A monastery is a controlled environment where this sort of emotional noise is kept to a minimum. No members of the opposite sex are allowed to live together there. Therefore, there is less opportunity for lust to arise. No possessions are allowed. Therefore, no ownership squabbles and less chance for greed and for coveting. Another hurdle for concentration should also be mentioned. In really deep concentration, you get so absorbed in the object of concentration that you forget all about trifles. Like your body, for instance, and your identity and everything around you. Here again the monastery is a useful convenience. It is nice to know that there is somebody to take care of you by watching over all the mundane matters of food and physical security. Without such assurance, one hesitates to go as deeply into concentration as one might. Mindfulness, on the other hand, is free from all these drawbacks. Mindfulness is not dependent on any such particular circumstance, physical or otherwise. It is a pure noticing factor. Thus it is free to notice whatever comes up—lust, hatred, or noise. Mindfulness is not limited by any condition. It exists to some extent in every moment, in every circumstance that arises. Also, mindfulness has no fixed object of focus. It observes change. Thus, it has an unlimited number of objects of attention. It just looks at whatever is passing through the mind and it does not categorize. Distractions and interruptions are noticed with the same amount of attention as the formal objects of meditation. In a state of pure mindfulness your attention just flows along with whatever changes are taking place in the mind. "Shift, shift, shift. Now this, now this, and now this."

You can't develop mindfulness by force. Active teeth-gritting willpower won't do you any good at all. As a matter of fact, it will hinder progress. Mindfulness cannot be cultivated by struggle. It grows by realizing, by letting go, by just settling down in the moment and letting yourself get comfortable with whatever you are experiencing. This does not mean that mindfulness happens all by itself. Far from it. Energy is required. Effort is required. But this effort is different from force. Mindfulness is cultivated by a gentle effort. The meditator cultivates mindfulness by constantly reminding himself in a gentle way to maintain his awareness of whatever is happening right now. Persistence and a light touch are the secrets. Mindfulness is cultivated by constantly pulling oneself back to a state of awareness, gently, gently, gently.

Mindfulness can't be used in any selfish way, either. It is egoless alertness. There is no "me" in a state of pure mindfulness. So there is no self to be selfish. On the contrary, it is mindfulness which gives you real perspective on yourself. It allows you to take that crucial mental step backward from your own desires and aversions so that you can then look and say, "Ah ha, so that's how I really am."

In a state of mindfulness, you see yourself exactly as you are. You see your own selfish behavior. You see your own suffering. And you see how you create that suffering. You see how you hurt others. You pierce right through the layer of lies that you normally tell yourself, and you see what is really there. Mindfulness leads to wisdom.

Mindfulness is not trying to achieve anything. It is just looking. Therefore, desire and aversion are not involved. Competition and struggle for achievement have no place in the process. Mindfulness does not aim at anything. It just sees whatever is already there.

Mindfulness is a broader and larger function than concentration. It is an all-encompassing function. Concentration is exclusive. It settles down on one item and ignores everything else. Mindfulness is inclusive. It stands back from the focus of attention and watches with a broad focus, quick to notice any change that occurs. If you have focused the mind on a stone, concentration will see only the stone. Mindfulness stands back from this process, aware of the stone, aware of concentration focusing on the stone, aware of the intensity of that focus and instantly aware of the shift of attention when concentration is distracted. It is mindfulness which notices that the distraction has occurred, and it is mindfulness which redirects the attention to the stone. Mindfulness is more difficult to cultivate than concentration because it is a deeper-reaching function. Concentration is merely focusing the mind, rather like a laser beam. It has the power to burn its way deep into the mind and illuminate what is there. But it does not understand what it sees. Mindfulness can examine the mechanics of selfishness and understand what it sees. Mindfulness can pierce the mystery of suffering and the mechanism of discomfort. Mindfulness can make you free.

There is, however, another Catch-22. Mindfulness does not react to what it sees. It just sees and understands. Mindfulness is the essence of patience. Therefore, whatever you see must simply be accepted, acknowledged, and dispassionately observed. This is not easy, but it is utterly necessary. We are ignorant. We are selfish and greedy and boastful. We lust, and we lie. These are facts. Mindfulness means seeing these facts and being patient with ourselves, accepting ourselves as we are. That goes against the grain. We don't want to accept it. We want to deny it. Or change it, or justify it. But acceptance is the essence of mindfulness. If we want to grow in mindfulness we must accept what mindfulness finds. It may be boredom, irritation, or fear. It may be weakness, inadequacy, or faults. Whatever it is, that is the way we are. That is what is real.

Mindfulness simply accepts whatever is there. If you want to grow in mindfulness, patient acceptance is the only route. Mindfulness grows only one way: by continuous practice of mindfulness, by simply trying to be mindful, and that means being patient. The process cannot be forced and it cannot be rushed. It proceeds at its own pace.

Concentration and mindfulness go hand in hand in the

job of meditation. Mindfulness directs the power of concentration. Mindfulness is the manager of the operation. Concentration furnishes the power by which mindfulness can penetrate into the deepest level of mind. Their cooperation results in insight and understanding. These must be cultivated together in a balanced manner. Just a bit more emphasis is given to mindfulness because mindfulness is the center of meditation. The deepest levels of concentration are not really needed to do the job of liberation. Still, a balance is essential. Too much awareness without calm to balance it will result in a wildly over-sensitized state similar to abusing LSD. Too much concentration without a balancing ratio of awareness will result in the "Stone Buddha" syndrome. The meditator gets so tranquilized that he sits there like a rock. Both of these are to be avoided.

The initial stages of mental cultivation are especially delicate. Too much emphasis on mindfulness at this point will actually retard the development of concentration. When getting started in meditation, one of the first things you will notice is how incredibly active the mind really is. The Theravada tradition calls this phenomenon "monkey mind." The Tibetan tradition likens it to a waterfall of thought. If you emphasize the awareness function at this point, there will be so much to be aware of that concentration will be impossible. Don't get discouraged. This happens to everybody. And there is a simple solution. Put most of your effort into one-pointedness at the beginning. Just keep calling the attention from wandering over and over again. Tough it out. Full instructions on how to do this are in Chapters 7 and 8. A couple of months down the track and you will have developed concentration power. Then you can start pumping your energy into mindfulness.

Do not, however, go so far with concentration that you find yourself going into a stupor.

Mindfulness still is the more important of the two components. It should be built as soon as you comfortably can do so. Mindfulness provides the needed foundation for the subsequent development of deeper concentration. Most blunders in this area of balance will correct themselves in time. Right concentration develops naturally in the wake of strong mindfulness. The more you develop the noticing factor, the quicker you will notice the distraction and the quicker you will pull out of it and return to the formal object of attention. The natural result is increased concentration. And as concentration develops, it assists the development of mindfulness. The more concentration power you have, the less chance there is of launching off on a long chain of analysis about the distraction. You simply note the distraction and return your attention to where it is supposed to be.

Thus the two factors tend to balance and support each other's growth quite naturally. Just about the only rule you need to follow at this point is to put your effort on concentration at the beginning, until the monkey mind phenomenon has cooled down a bit. After that, emphasize mindfulness. If you find yourself getting frantic, emphasize concentration. If you find yourself going into a stupor, emphasize mindfulness. Overall, mindfulness is the one to emphasize.

Mindfulness guides your development in meditation because mindfulness has the ability to be aware of itself. It is mindfulness which will give you a perspective on your practice. Mindfulness will let you know how you are doing. But don't worry too much about that. This is not a race. You are not in competition with anybody, and there is no schedule.

One of the most difficult things to learn is that mindfulness is not dependent on any emotional or mental state. We have certain images of meditation. Meditation is something done in quiet caves by tranquil people who move slowly. Those are training conditions. They are set up to foster concentration and to learn the skill of mindfulness. Once you have learned that skill, however, you can dispense with the training restrictions, and you should. You don't need to move at a snail's pace to be mindful. You don't even need to be calm. You can be mindful while solving problems in intensive calculus. You can be mindful in the middle of a football scrimmage. You can even be mindful in the midst of a raging fury. Mental and physical activities are no bar to mindfulness. If you find your mind extremely active, then simply observe the nature and degree of that activity. It is just a part of the passing show within.

# CHAPTER 15

# MEDITATION IN EVERYDAY LIFE

Every musician plays scales. When you begin to study the piano, that's the first thing you learn, and you never stop playing scales. The finest concert pianists in the world still play scales. It's a basic skill that can't be allowed to get rusty.

Every baseball player practices batting. It's the first thing you learn in Little League, and you never stop practicing. Every World Series game begins with batting practice. Basic skills must always remain sharp.

Seated meditation is the arena in which the meditator practices his own fundamental skills. The game the meditator is playing is the experience of his own life, and the instrument upon which he plays is his own sensory apparatus. Even the most seasoned meditator continues to practice seated meditation, because it tunes and sharpens the basic mental skills he needs for his particular game. We must never forget, however, that seated meditation itself is not the game. It's the practice. The game in which those basic skills are to be applied is the rest of one's experiential existence. Meditation that is not applied to daily living is sterile and limited.

The purpose of Vipassana meditation is nothing less than the radical and permanent transformation of your entire sensory and cognitive experience. It is meant to revolutionize the whole of your life experience. Those periods of seated practice are times set aside for instilling new mental habits.

You learn new ways to receive and understand sensation. You develop new methods of dealing with conscious thought, and new modes of attending to the incessant rush of your own emotions. These new mental behaviors must be made to carry over into the rest of your life. Otherwise, meditation remains dry and fruitless, a theoretical segment of your existence that is unconnected to all the rest. Some effort to connect these two segments is essential. A certain amount of carry-over will take place spontaneously, but that process will be slow and unreliable. You are very likely to be left with the feeling that you are getting nowhere and to drop the process as unrewarding.

One of the most memorable events in your meditation career is the moment when you first realize that you are meditating in the midst of a perfectly ordinary activity. You are driving down the freeway or carrying out the trash and it just turns on by itself. This unplanned outpouring of the skills you have been so carefully fostering is a genuine joy. It gives you a tiny window on the future. You catch a spontaneous glimpse of what the practice really means. The possibility strikes you that this transformation of consciousness could actually become a permanent feature of your experience. You realize that you could actually spend the rest of your days standing aside from the debilitating clamoring of your own obsessions, no longer frantically hounded by your own needs and greeds. You get a tiny taste of what it is like to just stand aside and watch it all flow past. It's a magic moment.

That vision is likely to remain unfulfilled, however, unless you actively seek to promote the carry-over process. The most important moment in meditation is the instant you leave the cushion. When your practice session is over, you can jump up and drop the whole thing, or you can bring those skills with you into the rest of your activities.

It is crucial for you to understand what meditation is. It is not some special posture, and it's not just a set of mental exercises. Meditation is the cultivation of mindfulness and the application of that mindfulness once cultivated. You do not have to sit to meditate. You can meditate while washing the dishes. You can meditate in the shower, or roller skating, or typing letters. Meditation is awareness, and it must be applied to each and every activity of one's life. This isn't easy.

We specifically cultivate awareness through the seated posture in a quiet place because that's the easiest situation in which to do so. Meditation in motion is harder. Meditation in the midst of fast-paced noisy activity is harder still. And meditation in the midst of intensely egoistic activities like romance or arguments is the ultimate challenge. The beginner will have his hands full with less stressful activities.

Yet the ultimate goal of practice remains: to build one's concentration and awareness to a level of strength that will remain unwavering even in the midst of the pressures of life in contemporary society. Life offers many challenges and the serious meditator is never bored.

Carrying your meditation into the events of your daily life is not a simple process. Try it and you will see. That transition point between the end of your meditation session and the beginning of "real life" is a long jump. It's too long for most of us. We find our calm and concentration evaporating within minutes, leaving us apparently no better off than before. In order to bridge this gulf, Buddhists over the centuries have devised an array of exercises aimed at smoothing the transition. They take that jump and break it down into little steps. Each step can be practiced by itself.

## WALKING MEDITATION

Our everyday existence is full of motion and activity. Sitting utterly motionless for hours on end is nearly the opposite of normal experience. Those states of clarity and tranquility we foster in the midst of absolute stillness tend to dissolve as soon as we move. We need some transitional exercise that will teach us the skill of remaining calm and aware in the midst of motion. Walking meditation helps us make that transition from static repose to everyday life. It's meditation in motion, and it is often used as an alternative to sitting. Walking is especially good for those times when you are extremely restless. An hour of walking meditation will often get you through that restless energy and still yield considerable quantities of clarity. You can then go on to the seated meditation with greater profit.

Standard Buddhist practice advocates frequent retreats to complement your daily sitting practice. A retreat is a relatively long period of time devoted exclusively to meditation. One or two day retreats are common for lay people. Seasoned meditators in a monastic situation may spend months at a time doing nothing else. Such practice is rigorous, and it makes sizable demands on both mind and body. Unless you have been at it for several years, there is a limit to how long you can sit and profit. Ten solid hours of the seated posture will produce in most beginners a state of agony that far exceeds their concentration powers. A profitable retreat must therefore be conducted with some change of posture and some movement. The usual pattern is to intersperse blocks of sitting with blocks of walking meditation. An hour of each with short breaks between is common.

To do the walking meditation, you need a private place

with enough space for at least five to ten paces in a straight line. You are going to be walking back and forth very slowly, and to the eyes of most Westerners, you'll look curious and disconnected from everyday life. This is not the sort of exercise you want to perform on the front lawn where you'll attract unnecessary attention. Choose a private place.

The physical directions are simple. Select an unobstructed area and start at one end. Stand for a minute in an attentive position. Your arms can be held in any way that is comfortable, in front, in back, or at your sides. Then while breathing in, lift the heel of one foot. While breathing out, rest that foot on its toes. Again while breathing in, lift that foot, carry it forward and while breathing out, bring the foot down and touch the floor. Repeat this for the other foot. Walk very slowly to the opposite end, stand for one minute, then turn around very slowly, and stand there for another minute before you walk back. Then repeat the process. Keep your head up and your neck relaxed. Keep your eyes open to maintain balance, but don't look at anything in particular. Walk naturally. Maintain the slowest pace that is comfortable, and pay no attention to your surroundings. Watch out for tensions building up in the body, and release them as soon as you spot them. Don't make any particular attempt to be graceful. Don't try to look pretty. This is not an athletic exercise, or a dance. It is an exercise in awareness. Your objective is to attain total alertness, heightened sensitivity and a full, unblocked experience of the motion of walking. Put all of your attention on the sensations coming from the feet and legs. Try to register as much information as possible about each foot as it moves. Dive into the pure sensation of walking, and notice every subtle nuance of the movement. Feel each individual muscle as it moves.

Experience every tiny change in tactile sensation as the feet press against the floor and then lift again. Notice the way these apparently smooth motions are composed of a complex series of tiny jerks. Try to miss nothing. In order to heighten your sensitivity, you can break the movement down into distinct components. Each foot goes through a lift, a swing, and then a down tread. Each of these components has a beginning, middle, and end. In order to tune yourself in to this series of motions, you can start by making explicit mental notes of each stage.

Make a mental note of "lifting, swinging, coming down, touching floor, pressing," and so on. This is a training procedure to familiarize you with the sequence of motions and to make sure that you don't miss any. As you become more aware of the myriad subtle events going on, you won't have time for words. You will find yourself immersed in a fluid, unbroken awareness of motion. The feet will become your whole universe. If your mind wanders, note the distraction in the usual way, then return your attention to walking. Don't look at your feet while you are doing all of this, and don't walk back and forth watching a mental picture of your feet and legs. Don't think, just feel. You don't need the concept of feet, and you don't need pictures. Just register the sensations as they flow. In the beginning, you will probably have some difficulties with balance. You are using the leg muscles in a new way, and a learning period is natural. If frustration arises, just note that and let it go.

The Vipassana walking technique is designed to flood your consciousness with simple sensations, and to do it so thoroughly that all else is pushed aside. There is no room for thought and therefore no room for emotion. There is no time for grasping and none for freezing the activity into a series of concepts. There is no need for a sense of self. There is only the sweep of tactile and kinesthetic sensation, an endless and ever-changing flood of raw experience. We are learning here to escape into reality, rather than from it. Whatever insights we gain are directly applicable to the rest of our notion-filled lives.

POSTURES

The goal of our practice is to become fully aware of all facets of our experience in an unbroken, moment-to-moment flow. Much of what we do and experience is completely unconscious in the sense that we do it with little or no attention. Our minds are on something else entirely. We spend most of our time running on automatic pilot, lost in the fog of daydreams and preoccupations.

One of the most frequently ignored aspects of our existence is our body. The technicolor cartoon show inside our head is so alluring that we tend to remove all of our attention from the kinesthetic and tactile senses. That information is pouring up the nerves and into the brain every second, but we have largely sealed it off from consciousness. It pours into the lower levels of the mind and it gets no further. Buddhists have developed an exercise to open the floodgates and let this material through to consciousness. It's another way of making the unconscious conscious.

Your body goes through all kinds of contortions in the course of a single day. You sit and you stand. You walk and lie down. You bend, run, crawl, and sprawl. Meditation teachers urge you to become aware of this constantly ongoing dance. As you go through your day, spend a few seconds every few minutes to check your posture. Don't do it in a judgmental way. This is not an exercise to correct your

177

posture, or to improve your appearance. Sweep your attention down through the body and feel how you are holding it. Make a silent mental note of "walking" or "sitting" or "lying down" or "standing." It all sounds absurdly simple, but don't slight this procedure. This is a powerful exercise. If you do it thoroughly, if you really instill this mental habit deeply, it can revolutionize your experience. It taps you into a whole new dimension of sensation, and you feel like a blind man whose sight has been restored.

## SLOW-MOTION ACTIVITY

Every action you perform is made up of separate components. The simple action of tying your shoelaces is made up of a complex series of subtle motions. Most of these details go unobserved. In order to promote the overall habit of mindfulness, you can perform simple activities at very low speed—making an effort to pay full attention to every nuance of the act.

Sitting at a table and drinking a cup of tea is one example. There is much here to be experienced. View your posture as you are sitting and feel the handle of the cup between your fingers. Smell the aroma of the tea, notice the placement of the cup, the tea, your arm, and the table. Watch the intention to raise the arm arise within your mind, feel the arm as it arises, feel the cup against your lip and liquid pouring into your mouth. Taste the tea, then watch the arising of the intention to lower your arm. The entire process is fascinating and beautiful, if you attend to it fully, paying detached attention to every sensation and to the flow of thought and emotion.

This same tactic can be applied to many of your daily activities. Intentionally slowing down your thoughts, words, and movements allows you to penetrate far more deeply into them than you otherwise could. What you find there is utterly astonishing. In the beginning, it is very difficult to keep this deliberately slow pace during most regular activities, but skill grows with time. Profound realizations occur during sitting meditation, but also profound revelations can take place when we really examine our own inner workings in the midst of day-to-day activities. This is the laboratory where we really start to see the mechanisms of our own emotions and the operations of our passions. Here is where we can truly gauge the reliability of our reasoning, and glimpse the difference between our true motives and that armor of pretense that we wear to fool ourselves and others.

We will find a great deal of this information surprising, much of it disturbing, but all of it useful. Bare attention brings order into the clutter that collects in those untidy little hidden corners of the mind. As you achieve clear comprehension in the midst of life's ordinary activities, you gain the ability to remain rational and peaceful while you throw the penetrating light of mindfulness into those irrational mental nooks and crannies. You start to see the extent to which you are responsible for your own mental suffering. You see your own miseries, fears, and tensions as self-generated. You see the way you cause your own suffering, weakness, and limitations. And the more deeply you understand these mental processes, the less hold they have on you.

BREATH COORDINATION

In seated meditation, our primary focus is the breath. Total concentration on the ever-changing breath brings us squarely into the present moment. The same principle can be used in the midst of movement. You can coordinate the activity in which you are involved with your breathing. This lends a flowing rhythm to your movement, and it smooths out many of the abrupt transitions. Activity becomes easier to focus on, and mindfulness is increased. Your awareness thus stays more easily in the present. Ideally, meditation should be a twenty-four hour-a-day practice. This is a highly practical suggestion.

A state of mindfulness is a state of mental readiness. The mind is not burdened with preoccupations or bound in worries. Whatever comes up can be dealt with instantly. When you are truly mindful, your nervous system has a freshness and resiliency which fosters insight. A problem arises, and you simply deal with it, quickly, efficiently, and with a minimum of fuss. You don't stand there in a dither, and you don't run off to a quiet corner so you can sit down and meditate about it. You simply deal with it. And in those rare circumstances when no solution seems possible, you don't worry about that. You just go on to the next thing that needs your attention. Your intuition becomes a very practical faculty.

STOLEN MOMENTS

The concept of wasted time does not exist for a serious meditator. Little dead spaces during your day can be turned to profit. Every spare moment can be used for meditation. Sitting anxiously in the dentist's office, meditate on your anxiety. Feeling irritated while standing in a line at the bank, meditate on irritation. Bored, twiddling your thumbs at the bus stop, meditate on boredom. Try to stay alert and aware throughout the day. Be mindful of exactly what is taking place right now, even if it is tedious drudgery. Take advantage of moments when you are alone. Take advantage of activities that are largely mechanical. Use every spare second to be mindful. Use all the moments you can.

## CONCENTRATION ON ALL ACTIVITIES

You should try to maintain mindfulness of every activity and perception through the day, starting with the first perception when you awake, and ending with the last thought before you fall asleep. This is an incredibly tall goal to shoot for. Don't expect to be able to achieve this work soon. Just take it slowly and let your abilities grow over time. The most feasible way to go about the task is to divide your day up into chunks. Dedicate a certain interval to mindfulness of posture, then extend this mindfulness to other simple activities: eating, washing, dressing, and so forth. Some time during the day, you can set aside fifteen minutes or so to practice the observation of specific types of mental states: pleasant, unpleasant, and neutral feelings, for instance; or the hindrances, or thoughts. The specific routine is up to you. The idea is to get practice at spotting the various items, and to preserve your state of mindfulness as fully as you can throughout the day.

Try to achieve a daily routine in which there is as little difference as possible between seated meditation and the rest of your experience. Let the one slide naturally into the other. Your body is almost never still. There is always motion to observe. At the very least, there is breathing. Your mind never stops chattering, except in the very deepest states of concentration. There is always something coming up to observe. If you seriously apply your meditation, you will never be at a loss for something worthy of your attention.

Your practice must be made to apply to your everyday living situation. That is your laboratory. It provides the trials and challenges you need to make your practice deep and genuine. It's the fire that purifies your practice of deception and error, the acid test that shows you when you are getting somewhere and when you are fooling yourself. If your meditation isn't helping you to cope with everyday conflicts and struggles, then it is shallow. If your day-to-day emotional reactions are not becoming clearer and easier to manage, then you are wasting your time. And you never know how you are doing until you actually make that test.

The practice of mindfulness is supposed to be a universal practice. You don't do it sometimes and drop it the rest of the time. You do it all the time. Meditation that is successful only when you are withdrawn in some soundproof ivory tower is still undeveloped. Insight meditation is the practice of moment-to-moment mindfulness. The meditator learns to pay bare attention to birth, growth, and decay of all the phenomena of the mind. He turns from none of it, and he lets none of it escape. This includes thoughts and emotions, activities and desires, the whole show. He watches it all and he watches it continuously. It matters not whether it is lovely or horrid, beautiful or shameful. He sees the way it is and the way it changes. No aspect of experience is excluded or avoided. It is a very thoroughgoing procedure.

If you are moving through your daily activities and you find yourself in a state of boredom, then meditate on your boredom. Find out how it feels, how it works, and what it is composed of. If you are angry, meditate on the anger. Explore the mechanics of anger. Don't run from it. If you find yourself sitting in the grip of a dark depression, meditate on that depression. Investigate depression in a detached and inquiring way. Don't flee from it blindly. Explore the maze and chart its pathways. That way you will be better able to cope with the next depression that comes along.

Meditating your way through the ups and downs of daily life is the whole point of Vipassana. This kind of practice is extremely rigorous and demanding, but it engenders a state of mental flexibility that is beyond comparison. A meditator keeps his mind open every second. He is constantly investigating life, inspecting his own experience, viewing existence in a detached and inquisitive way. Thus, he is constantly open to truth in any form, from any source, and at any time. This is the state of mind you need for Liberation.

It is said that one may attain Enlightenment at any moment if the mind is kept in a state of meditative readiness. The tiniest, most ordinary perception can be the stimulus: a view of the moon, the cry of a bird, the sound of the wind in the trees. It's not so important what is perceived as the way in which you attend to that perception. That state of open readiness is essential. It could happen to you right now if you are ready. The tactile sensation of this book in your fingers could be the cue. The sound of these words in your head might be enough. You could attain Enlightenment right now, if you are ready.

# CHAPTER 16

## WHAT'S IN IT FOR YOU

You can expect certain benefits from your meditation. The initial ones are practical things; the later stages are profoundly transcendental. They run together from the simple to the sublime. We will set forth some of them here. Your own practice can show you the truth. Your own experience is all that counts.

Those things that we called hindrances or defilements are more than just unpleasant mental habits. They are the primary manifestations of the ego process itself. The ego sense itself is essentially a feeling of separation—a perception of distance between that which we call me, and that which we call other. This perception is held in place only if it is constantly exercised, and the hindrances constitute that exercise.

Greed and lust are attempts to get "some of that" for me; hatred and aversion are attempts to place greater distance between "me and that." All the defilements depend upon the perception of a barrier between self and other, and all of them foster this perception every time they are exercised. Mindfulness perceives things deeply and with great clarity. It brings our attention to the root of the defilements and lays bare their mechanism. It sees their fruits and their effects upon us. It cannot be fooled. Once you have clearly seen what greed really is and what it really does to you and to others, you just naturally cease to engage in it. When a child burns his hand on a hot oven, you don't have to tell him to pull it back; he does it naturally, without conscious thought and without decision. There is a reflex action built into the nervous system for just that purpose, and it works faster than thought. By the time the child perceives the sensation of heat and begins to cry, the hand has already been jerked back from the source of pain. Mindfulness works in very much the same way: it is wordless, spontaneous, and utterly efficient. Clear mindfulness inhibits the growth of hindrances; continuous mindfulness extinguishes them. Thus, as genuine mindfulness is built up, the walls of the ego itself are broken down, craving diminishes, defensiveness and rigidity lessen, you become more open, accepting, and flexible. You learn to share your loving kindness.

Traditionally, Buddhists are reluctant to talk about the ultimate nature of human beings. But those who are willing to make descriptive statements at all usually say that our ultimate essence or Buddha nature is pure, holy, and inherently good. The only reason that human beings appear otherwise is that their experience of that ultimate essence has been hindered; it has been blocked like water behind the dam. The hindrances are the bricks of which that dam is built. As mindfulness dissolves the bricks, holes are punched in the dam, and compassion and sympathetic joy come flooding forward. As meditative mindfulness develops, your whole experience of life changes. Your experience of being alive, the very sensation of being conscious, becomes lucid and precise, no longer just an unnoticed background for your preoccupations. It becomes a thing consistently perceived.

Each passing moment stands out as itself; the moments no longer blend together in an unnoticed blur. Nothing is glossed over or taken for granted, no experiences labeled as merely "ordinary." Everything looks bright and special. You refrain from categorizing your experiences into mental pigeonholes. Descriptions and interpretations are chucked aside, and each moment of time is allowed to speak for itself. You actually listen to what it has to say, and you listen as if it were being heard for the very first time. When your meditation becomes really powerful, it also becomes constant. You consistently observe with bare attention both the breath and every mental phenomenon. You feel increasingly stable, increasingly moored in the stark and simple experience of moment-to-moment existence.

Once your mind is free from thought, it becomes clearly wakeful and at rest in an utterly simple awareness. This awareness cannot be described adequately. Words are not enough. It can only be experienced. Breath ceases to be just breath; it is no longer limited to the static and familiar concept you once held. You no longer see it as a succession of just inhalations and exhalations; it is no longer an insignificant monotonous experience. Breath becomes a living, changing process, something alive and fascinating. It is no longer something that takes place in time; it is perceived as the present moment itself. Time is seen as a concept, not an experienced reality.

This is a simplified, rudimentary awareness which is stripped of all extraneous detail. It is grounded in a living flow of the present, and it is marked by a pronounced sense of reality. You know absolutely that this is real, more real than anything you have ever experienced. Once you have gained this perception with absolute certainty, you have a fresh vantage point, a new criterion against which to gauge all of your experience. After this perception, you see clearly those moments when you are participating in bare phenomena alone, and those moments when you are disturbing phenomena with mental attitudes. You watch yourself twisting reality with mental comments, with stale images and personal opinions. You know what you are doing, when you are doing it. You become increasingly sensitive to the ways in which you miss the true reality, and you gravitate toward the simple objective perspective which does not add to or subtract from what is. You become a very perceptive individual. From this vantage point, all is seen with clarity. The innumerable activities of mind and body stand out in glaring detail. You mindfully observe the incessant rise and fall of breath; you watch an endless stream of bodily sensations and movements; you scan the rapid succession of thoughts and feelings, and you sense the rhythm that echoes from the steady march of time. And in the midst of all this ceaseless movement, there is no watcher, there is only watching.

In this state of perception, nothing remains the same for two consecutive moments. Everything is seen to be in constant transformation. All things are born, all things grow old and die. There are no exceptions. You awaken to the unceasing changes of your own life. You look around and see everything in flux, everything, everything, everything. It is all rising and falling, intensifying and diminishing, coming into existence and passing away. All of life, every bit of it from the infinitesimal to the Pacific Ocean, is in motion constantly. You perceive the universe as a great flowing river of experience. Your most cherished possessions are slipping away, and so is your very life. Yet this impermanence is no reason for grief. You stand there transfixed, staring at this incessant activity, and your response is wondrous joy. It's all moving, dancing, and full of life.

As you continue to observe these changes and you see how it all fits together, you become aware of the intimate connectedness of all mental, sensory, and affective phenomena. You watch one thought leading to another, you see destruction giving rise to emotional reactions and feelings giving rise to more thoughts. Actions, thoughts, feelings, desires— you see all of them intimately linked together in a delicate fabric of cause and effect. You watch pleasurable experiences arise and fall and you see that they never last; you watch pain come uninvited and you watch yourself anxiously struggling to throw it off; you see yourself fail. It all happens over and over while you stand back quietly and just watch it all work.

Out of this living laboratory itself comes an inner and unassailable conclusion. You see that your life is marked by disappointment and frustration, and you clearly see the source. These reactions arise out of your own inability to get what you want, your fear of losing what you have already gained, and your habit of never being satisfied with what you have. These are no longer theoretical concepts— you have seen these things for yourself and you know that they are real. You perceive your own fear, your own basic insecurity in the face of life and death. It is a profound tension that goes all the way down to the root of thought and makes all of life a struggle. You watch yourself anxiously groping about, fearfully grasping after solid, trustworthy ground. You see yourself endlessly grasping for something, anything, to hold onto in the midst of all these shifting sands, and you see that there is nothing to hold onto, nothing that doesn't change.

You see the pain of loss and grief, you watch yourself being forced to adjust to painful developments day after day in your own ordinary existence. You witness the tensions and conflicts inherent in the very process of everyday living, and you see how superficial most of your concerns really are. You watch the progress of pain, sickness, old age, and death. You learn to marvel that all these horrible things are not fearful at all. They are simply reality.

Through this intensive study of the negative aspects of your existence, you become deeply acquainted with *dukkha,* the unsatisfactory nature of all existence. You begin to perceive *dukkha* at all levels of our human life, from the obvious down to the most subtle. You see the way suffering inevitably follows in the wake of clinging, as soon as you grasp anything, pain inevitably follows. Once you become fully acquainted with the whole dynamic of desire, you become sensitized to it. You see where it rises, when it rises, and how it affects you. You watch it operate over and over, manifesting through every sense channel, taking control of the mind and making consciousness its slave.

In the midst of every pleasant experience, you watch your own craving and clinging take place. In the midst of unpleasant experiences, you watch a very powerful resistance take hold. You do not block these phenomena, you just watch them; you see them as the very stuff of human thought. You search for that thing you call "me," but what you find is a physical body and how you have identified your sense of yourself with that bag of skin and bones. You search further, and you find all manner of mental phenomena, such as emotions, thought patterns, and opinions, and see how you identify the sense of yourself with each of them. You watch yourself becoming possessive, protective, and defensive over these pitiful things, and you see how crazy that is. You rummage furiously among these various items, constantly searching for yourself—physical matter, bodily sensations, feelings, and emotions—it all keeps whirling round and round as you root through it, peering into every nook and cranny, endlessly hunting for "me."

You find nothing. In all that collection of mental hardware in this endless stream of ever-shifting experience all you can find is innumerable impersonal processes which have been caused and conditioned by previous processes. There is no static self to be found; it is all process. You find thoughts but no thinker, you find emotions and desires, but nobody doing them. The house itself is empty. There is nobody home.

Your whole view of self changes at this point. You begin to look upon yourself as if you were a newspaper photograph. When viewed with the naked eyes, the photograph you see is a definite image. When viewed through a magnifying glass, it all breaks down into an intricate configuration of dots. Similarly, under the penetrating gaze of mindfulness, the feeling of a self, an "I" or "being" anything, loses its solidity and dissolves. There comes a point in insight meditation where the three characteristics of existence—impermanence, unsatisfactoriness, and selflessness—come rushing home with concept-searing force. You vividly experience the impermanence of life, the suffering nature of human existence, and the truth of no-self. You experience these things so graphically that you suddenly awake to the utter futility of craving, grasping, and resistance. In the clarity and purity of this profound moment, our consciousness is transformed. The entity of self evaporates. All that is left is an infinity of interrelated non-personal phenomena, which are conditioned and ever-changing. Craving is extinguished and a great burden is lifted. There remains only an effortless flow, without a trace of resistance or tension. There remains only peace, and blessed Nibbana, the uncreated, is realized.

# ABOUT THE AUTHOR

Venerable Henepola Gunaratana was ordained at the age of twelve as a Buddhist monk in Malandeniya, Sri Lanka. In 1947, at age twenty, he was given higher ordination in Kandy. He received his education from Vidyalankara College and Buddhist Missionary College in Colombo. Subsequently he travelled to India for five years of missionary work for the Mahabodhi Society, serving the *harijana* (untouchable) people in Sanchi, Delhi, and Bombay. Later he spent ten years as a missionary in Malaysia, serving as religious advisor to the Sasana Abhivurdhiwardhana Society, the Buddhist Missionary Society, and the Buddhist Youth Federation of Malaysia. He has been a teacher in Kishon Dial School and Temple Road Girls' School, and principal of the Buddhist Institute of Kuala Lumpur.

At the invitation of the Sasana Sevaka Society, he came to the United States in 1968 to serve as general secretary of the Buddhist Vihara Society of Washington, D.C. In 1980, he was appointed president of the Society. During his years at the vihara, he taught courses in Buddhism, conducted meditation retreats, and lectured widely throughout the United States, Canada, Europe, Australia, and New Zealand.

He has also pursued his scholarly interests by earning a Ph.D. degree in philosophy from The American University. He has taught courses on Buddhism at The American University, Georgetown University, and the University of Maryland. His books and articles have been published in Malaysia, India, Sri Lanka, and the United States.

Since 1973, Venerable Gunaratana has been Buddhist chaplain at The American University. He is now president of the Bhavana Society in the Shenandoah Valley of West Virginia.

# WISDOM PUBLICATIONS

W isdom Publications is a non-profit publisher of books on Buddhism, Tibet, and related East-West themes. Our titles are published in appreciation of Buddhism as a living philosophy and with the special commitment to preserve and transmit important works from all the major Buddhist traditions.

If you would like more information or a copy of our extensive mail order catalogue, and to keep informed about future publications, please write to us at: 361 Newbury Street, Boston, Massachusetts, 02115, USA.

Wisdom is a non-profit, charitable 501(c)(3) organization and a part of the Foundation for the Preservation of the Mahayana Tradition (FPMT).

# CARE OF DHARMA BOOKS

DHARMA BOOKS contain the teachings of the Buddha; they have the power to protect against lower rebirth and to point the way to liberation. Therefore, they should be treated with respect—kept off the floor and places where people sit or walk—and not stepped over. They should be covered or protected for transporting and kept in a high, clean place separate from more "mundane" materials. Other objects should not be placed on top of Dharma books and materials. Licking the fingers to turn pages is considered bad form (and negative karma). If it is necessary to dispose of Dharma materials, they should be burned rather than thrown in the trash. When burning Dharma, first recite OM, AH, HUNG. Then, visualize the letters of the texts (to be burned) absorbing into the AH, and that absorbing into you. After that, you can burn the texts.

These considerations may also be kept in mind for Dharma artwork, as well as the written teachings and artwork of other religions.

## HOW TO MEDITATE

*A Practical Guide*
Kathleen McDonald
Edited by Robina Courtin

What is meditation? Why practice it? Which technique is best for me? How do I do it? The answers to these often-asked questions are contained in this down-to-earth book, compiled and written by Kathleen McDonald, a Western Buddhist nun with solid experience in both the practice and teaching of meditation. *How to Meditate* contains a wealth of practical advice on a variety of authentic and proven techniques.

"An excellent introduction ... refreshingly readable ... clarity without oversimplification." —*Buddhist Studies Review*

"This book is as beautifully simple and direct as its title ... earnestly recommended." —*Yoga Today*

$10.95, paper, 224 pp., ISBN 0-86171-009-6

# THE FINE ARTS
## OF RELAXATION, CONCENTRATION AND MEDITATION
*Ancient Skills for Modern Minds*
Joel and Michelle Levey

This practical workbook presents more than one hundred techniques for mastering the stress of life. The Leveys have drawn from the humanistic psychotherapies, Zen, Tibetan Buddhism, Christianity, Judaism, and other tried and proven systems. They show that it is definitely possible, with even a little knowledge of the fine arts of relaxation, concentration and meditation, to reduce stress, improve relationships and generally enhance the quality of our lives.

"Skillfully weaves together contemporary insights into the value and need for meditation in our lives with a large number of extremely evocative suggestions for different ways to practice." —Jon Kabat-Zinn, author of *Wherever You Go, There You Are* and *Full Catastrophe Living*

"*The Fine Arts* is a skillful blend of time-proven antidotes to the stress of modern life." —Dan Goleman, author of *The Meditative Mind* and *New York Times* Psychology writer

$14.95, paper, 232 pp., ISBN 0-86171-040-1

BEING NOBODY, GOING NOWHERE
*Meditations on the Buddhist Path*
Ayya Khema

Ayya Khema, a Western Buddhist nun, describes simple and effective meditation methods for developing calm and insight, for expanding feelings of loving kindness and compassion towards others, and for overcoming obstacles to practice. Written with pure sincerity and strength, this is a simple yet inspiring book. The techniques Ayya Khema describes can be understood and practiced by everybody.

"This book is a valuable guide to the path of meditative insight and living compassion. It is direct, clear and inspiring." —Sharon Salzberg, co-founder of the Insight Meditation Society, Barre, Massachusetts

$12.95, paper, 192 pp., ISBN 0-86171-052-5


INTRODUCTION TO TANTRA
*A Vision of Totality*
Lama Yeshe
Compiled and edited by Jonathan Landaw

Lama Yeshe brings to life and makes clear the often misunderstood ideas of tantra. He explains that normally our desires bring us only more dissatisfaction, but if used skillfully, they can help break down our distorted way of seeing things. He shows clearly how tantra fits within the framework of conventional Buddhist practices, such as karma, renunciation, and compassion, emphasizing compassion for others as the driving force of all Buddhist practice.

"No one has ever talked about Tantra with such clarity, coherence and simplicity. ... No one has summarized the essence so well." —*Religious Studies Review*

$12.95, paper, 176 pp., ISBN 0-86171-021-5


*These and other Dharma books are available from Wisdom Publications. To place your credit card order call 1-800-272-4050.*